INTRINSIC
FREEDOM

Intrinsic Freedom is a delightful book bringing together the ancient teachings of Buddhism and the thoroughly up-to-date concerns of the modern reader. The Fenners present a simple, yet profound, definition of stress. They show why our usual attempts to resolve stress through techniques and self-improvement strategies are inevitably ineffectual. The Fenners point, instead, to "presence," our natural state of being which is already spacious and free from stress. I heartily recommend this creative and provocative book which offers us challenging insight into how we usually live our lives.

Karen Kissel Wegela, Ph.D.
Director of the Contemplative Psychotherapy Program
Naropa Institute

This book offers clear and practical wisdom for anyone wanting to reduce stress and understand the function of belief in shaping perception. It is easy to read, and the ideas are simple yet profound in their implications.

Frances E. Vaughan, Ph.D.
Psychologist
Author of *The Inward Arc* and Co-author of *Beyond Ego*

Dr. Peter Fenner brings a rather extraordinary background to this book. Combining his extensive practice as a Buddhist monk with his studies of Western philosophy has led to a remarkable work which sheds new light on the sources of stress in modern life. The book is especially persuasive in demonstrating how our deep beliefs, many of which are not even visible to ourselves, shape our lives and our perception of reality. This work will be of significant benefit to anyone who has a sincere interest in personal growth and development.

David H. Goldberg, Ph.D.
Dean, Graduate School of Holistic Studies
John F. Kennedy University

INTRINSIC FREEDOM

THE ART OF STRESS-FREE LIVING

PETER FENNER

with Penny Fenner

MILLENNIUM BOOKS

First published in 1994 by
Millennium Books
an imprint of E.J. Dwyer (Australia) Pty Ltd
3/32–72 Alice Street
Newtown NSW 2042
Australia
Phone: (02) 550–2355
Fax: (02) 519–3218

National Library of Australia
Cataloguing-in-Publication data

Fenner, Peter G., 1949– .
Intrinsic freedom: the art of stress-free living.

Includes index.
ISBN 1 86429 000 5

1. Stress management. 2. Self (Philosophy). 3. Self-actualization (Psychology). I. Fenner, Penny, 1954– . II. Title.

Edited by Shelley Neller
Cover design by Reno, Sydney
Text design by Nicole Matthews
Typeset in 11/13 Schneidler Old Style by DOCUPRO, Sydney
Printed in Australia by Australian Print Group

10 9 8 7 6 5 4 3 2 1
98 97 96 95 94

FOREWORD

I first met Peter Fenner over the telephone in the middle of summer, 1991. One evening my phone rang and an Australian accent came through—"Peter Fenner here, calling from Australia." A mutual friend had given Peter my name.

After some 'kibitzing' and introductory exchanges, Peter asked me if I might be willing to arrange for him to speak at Psychiatric Grand Rounds at Stanford in the winter of 1992 when he would be in California on a lecture tour. I asked Peter what his topic would be, and he said: "Oh, I don't know—perhaps something like the 'Buddhist notion of presence.'" I said: "The Buddhist notion of presence? Peter, are you sure? Do you know who your audience will be? They'll chew you up!" There was a pregnant pause from his end of the line, and then he said slowly: "Well then I guess I'll have the experience of being chewed up." I laughed deeply and without cognitively knowing it, I had an experience of what Peter meant by *presence*.

He possessed a light, almost lithe quality that made me smile and feel relaxed. I felt I could be entirely candid and open with Peter although I had just met him. There was something unencumbered about his vibration which signaled to me that it was absolutely all right to be whoever I was at the moment. His perspective seemed completely accepting and I felt a tremendous amount of space. Only later, after reading *Intrinsic Freedom*, did I come to realize that this quality in Peter is what the Fenners term "spaciousness."

Penny Fenner portrayed this quality also. When I first met Penny it was as though we started our conversation in the middle of a paragraph—it seemed like a continuation of dialogue that we had started at some previous meeting. There was no pretense, nothing to prove, nothing to win, no resistance. What seemed to exist was flow, a playful volley of energy and interesting ideas and a space that could contain whatever I created.

I learned that Peter was a philosopher who had been a Buddhist monk for nine years. He was devoutly interested in melding the philosophies of the East with those of the West, both of which he has studied rigorously. Penny, a psychologist, had been a student of Buddhism for many years and had previously been married to a Tibetan lama. Peter and Penny had been involved in establishing Buddhist communities in Australia and were now dedicating a major portion of their lives to bringing some of the most powerful wisdom teachings of the East to the "Western mind." I learned that they had developed a practical course that extracted the cream of Buddhist teachings, condensed this and reframed it so that it was readily digestible for a Western mind. I also learned that they were writing a book called *Intrinsic Freedom* that illustrated some of the foundational dynamics and major teachings of the practical course.

After studying the framework presented in *Intrinsic Freedom*, I experienced the practical course. *Intrinsic Freedom* is an outline or framework about "spaciousness" the true freedom of being; and "natural release"—the evaporation of limiting beliefs and constricting emotions into nothing. It is a valuable map to serenity, peace of mind, and the ability to live without stress. This book is the "what" of these phenomena, while the course is a practicum in the "how."

Their new model distills thousands of years of ancient wisdom teachings and synthesizes them into a modern paradigm for dealing with dissatisfaction and conflict. This model presents the possibility of moment-by-moment fulfillment genuinely free of burdensome thoughts and conflicting emotions. It cuts through the illusions that one can be somewhere different from where one is or someone other than who one is.

Intrinsic Freedom offers the reader a simple yet extremely powerful alternative to the change model of modern psychotherapy. The change model implies that something is broken or wrong—otherwise why would one be trying to fix or alter it? *Intrinsic Freedom* encourages one to just see what's there and allow it to be. When you look at a forest, which leaf is in the wrong place? Each leaf is exactly where it should be, given the current situation—right? *Intrinsic Freedom* suggests that the same is true of our psyches—our thoughts and our feelings are just as they should be, given our histories, conditioning, and so forth. In trying to alter or control our feelings and thoughts, we actually create problems for ourselves. Paradoxically, by allowing things to be, we create the space for evolution and freedom.

Stress is defined by the Fenners as what occurs when there

is a difference (a delta) between what is and what we believe we want to be so, or what we believe should be so. More often than not, in the West, we try to change or control what's so. With the practice of natural release, one neutralizes and lets go of beliefs, thoughts and feelings about how something "shoulda, coulda, oughta" be and is able to simply be with what is.

By "being with" one's feelings and thoughts, the stress of thinking that these thoughts and feelings should be or could be otherwise, disappears. Most of the pain or discomfort of dreaded feelings comes not from the feelings themselves, but from the avoidance of or resistance to the feelings. A spaciousness occurs when one no longer dreads and resists his or her feelings and thoughts. When one allows, becomes present to, and embraces one's thoughts and feelings, an inner serenity and an outer freshness blow in.

How many hours and dollars have you spent on trying to change yourself? Has it been successful? *Intrinsic Freedom* offers a very different map to peace of mind, a map that doesn't judge anything as wrong or out of place; it's just the way it is and if it could be otherwise, it would be—just like the leaves on the trees. If you're tired of trying to change or control your feelings, this model offers you an alternative. It's simple, it's elegant, it's ineffable, and it makes no ordinary sense.

The Fenners have spent thousands of hours in the deepest layers of their own psyches. They have spent long periods of time in places that most of us barely visit for moments. If I use a computer analogy, they have worked at the level of the chip, while most of us spend our time looking at the monitor. In other words, the Fenners' system works at the level of the projector where the images are actually created, whereas most change models try to affect the images on the screen. By being at the place of projection (creation) of thoughts and feelings, we take ownership, we are at cause; we are the source of our perceptions rather than merely being reactive to the projections which show up on the screen. Mastery accompanies the experience of being at source and peace of mind accompanies the experience of mastery.

The building blocks presented in *Intrinsic Freedom* are simple yet profoundly penetrating when genuinely experienced. The key principles include the insights that a) beliefs arise in pairs of complements; b) stress, conflict and alienation are caused by conflicting beliefs; and c) these conflicting beliefs can be harmonized by naturally releasing the energy that keeps conflicting beliefs disconnected. For example, when we realize and experience that we are attracted to what is repulsive and love what we find contemptuous, a great release occurs.

I know this sounds absurd when heard at the level at which most of us process information. However, when we move to the deeper levels of consciousness—to the quiet layers of the mind which we can access by being very still for some time—this is what we find. By bringing together what appears to be oppositional, we release great amounts of energy which can be used for creative purposes rather than being used to separate and divide our worlds.

Peter finally did present some of the wisdom in *Intrinsic Freedom* to Psychiatric Grand Rounds at Stanford. If there was any "chewing up" occurring, I'd have to say it was done by Peter. He took one assumption of psychotherapy after another, and demonstrated how it helped avoid the immediacy of the present experience.

It was then that I knew there was something profound for me to learn from Peter Fenner. I saw a room full of scholars and masters of the mind, baffled, perplexed, and finally more spacious. Perplexed, not because Dr. Fenner was being unclear . . . Perplexed in the best sense of the word . . . Perplexed because they were being confronted with a whole new way of creating well-being. As most have experienced, this kind of perplexity leads to growth and integration if one is secure and willing to challenge one's current structure of belief.

My wish for you, the reader, is that you too become perplexed upon reading this wonderful book. After perplexity comes spaciousness! Enjoy!

Gary G. Lapid M.D.
Associate Clinical Professor of
Psychiatry and Behavioral Sciences
Stanford University School of Medicine
Stanford, California.

DEDICATION

This book is dedicated to the memory and inspiration of Lama Thubten Yeshe and Lama Thukse Rinpoche.

ACKNOWLEDGEMENTS

We are grateful to Dr. Gary Lapid for his generous Foreword and enthusiastic support of our work. We thank Drs. Karen Kissel Wegela, Bill McLeod and Rob McNeilly for providing helpful feedback on earlier drafts of the book. We also thank our course participants. Their experiences have allowed us to refine our work through an elegant cycle in which theory and implementation have transformed each other. Finally we thank Catherine Hammond, our editor at Millennium, for her enthusiastic and professional support.

CONTENTS

Contents

PREFACE

Writing this book has been different from others I have authored. For a number of years I have had a strong sense that my intense study and practice of the Asian wisdom traditions would "come together" one day as a simple system of theory and practical exercises. However, I didn't know when this would happen.

Towards the end of 1991 two or three important insights allowed me to integrate the most valuable philosphical perspectives I had studied and practiced over the last twenty years or so. I was also able to see how this newly emerging framework could be applied through a series of practical exercises. Once this had happened, the writing of this book and the development of the course that accompanies it flowed easily. In fact, it has been a delight to express the essence of well-being as I understand it.

The result is a synthesis of my richest experiences and deepest understanding of the world's wisdom traditions.

When I reflect on my life, it is clear to me that a number of events and experiences have contributed to the emergence of this work. Perhaps the first formative experience occurred when I was seven, living in Adelaide, Australia. Like a good boy in a WASPish family, I went to Sunday school each week. I enjoyed the stories and drawings we did. Then one week we were introduced to the Ten Commandments. Immediately on hearing the third commandment I began to blaspheme quietly to myself. As each minute went by, I found myself unwittingly and uncontrollably doing exactly what I had been told never to do.

The words "God is a bugger" spun obsessively in my mind like a sacred mantra. I lay awake at night, unable to clear my mind of these uncontrollable words. I became terrified. Each time I uttered my incantation, I sank deeper into a state of terror and fear of the inevitable outcome I was creating in committing such a sin. Yet I could not stop myself. It seemed as though I were already in hell. After about two days, I plucked up enough courage to confess my evil doings to my mother. Her response amazed me and produced in me my first profound realization.

Rather than berating me, or warning me of the dire consequences that must ensue from such obsessive sinning, she quite simply told me not to worry about it. "Don't worry!" she said and immediately my pain and anguish were relieved. Within seconds I was floating. I was released from my deepest fears and experienced a profound sense of peace and tranquillity.

Thus, at an early age I realized just how powerful the game of religion can be in our culture. Not surprisingly, from then on I couldn't relate at all to doctrinal religion. Orthodox Christianity lost any meaning it had had for me. More significantly, though, I had directly experienced the power of language and thoughts and seen how heaven and hell can be mental creations.

My experience of the power of the mind matured through my early teens into a serious interest in mysticism. This interest was also stimulated by odd experiences I began to have when I was about fourteen. Each night for a period of about two months I would experience my body-image either expanding or contracting to a point where I feared my identity would completely dissolve. These experiences frightened and confused me but they also led me to the writings of Christian mystics such as St. John of the Cross, St. Teresa and Meister Eckhardt. I felt a deep affinity for the renunciative life and longed for the experience of the Godhead that Eckhardt wrote about. The more I read, the more I knew that our waking reality was not all there was to life.

Shortly after leaving school I experimented with mind-altering drugs and this paved the way for taking up philosophical and religious studies at university. The experience of reality dissolving before my eyes opened me to the perennial philosophical inquiry as to what is and isn't real.

At university I specialised in the disciplines of ontology and epistemology—the study of "what is real" and "how we know." I also studied philosophy of mind. The rigorous intellectual study gave me provisional frameworks for understanding the experiences I was acquiring through drugs. Drugs, as it were, provided base raw material with which to explore the validity of the philosophical and logical tools I was acquiring.

These were heady days. I was living on the edge of sanity and transcendence. During this period I also experimented with the opiates which stimulate an extreme range of somatic sensations. With these I experienced physical bliss and also the hell of addiction and withdrawal. Whilst I had success in understanding the internal logic and structure of the drug-induced experiences, I struggled to keep my feet on the ground. Drugs became destructive and confusing. I needed a more mature way to continue my study of what is real.

At this same time—and as a radical correction to my experiments with drugs—I became a father. The period preceding the birth of my daughter was one of the most difficult in my life. I had tasted the bliss and freedom of the non-dualistic experience that the mystics speak about, and in the process I had become very ungrounded. The physical world had become very unreal and I was disconnected from the necessities of daily living. However, my new commitment to being a father in the fullest sense was just as strong as my commitment to discovering the ultimate nature of reality. This new commitment led me through my own dark side, or shadow, as I struggled to let go of the mystical visions that I so highly prized.

At this time I began to study Indian and other Eastern traditions which explored reality and the nature of the mind through meditative practices. As always my study was accompanied by practice—this time through the discipline of meditation. Initially I began by following instructions I read in books on Buddhist meditation. Soon afterwards I connected with a Theravada Buddhist group and attended some retreats.

In 1974 I met the Tibetan teachers, Lama Thubten Yeshe and Lama Thubten Zopa Rinpoche. They had been invited to Australia by students who had attended their meditation courses in Nepal. As did many others, I connected with Lama Yeshe immediately. He exuded all the qualities I associated with true spiritual insight and understanding—presence, fearlessness, compassion, spontaneity, joy and personal power. I was drawn to him and the following year I formally asked him to be my guru. He accepted.

Though I was married at the time with one child, I also requested Lama Yeshe to ordain me as a monk. I wasn't one for half-hearted commitments. I was serious. I wanted nirvana in this life and I wanted it while living in a Western domestic environment. In any normal circumstances this would not have been possible. There was no precedent in the Tibetan monastic tradition for ordination while married and living in a domestic situation, but Lama Yeshe said: "Yes, if this is what you want I can arrange it for you."

However, before doing this he agreed with my wife that we should have one more child. So we returned home, and conceived our second daughter. I then travelled to Nepal and later to India where I was ordained into a Tibetan Buddhist order at a monastery in South India. The abbot of the monastery gave me the name Ngawang Tharpa which means "Liberating through Powerful Speech."

I returned to Australia to a unique situation. I lived with my family and also kept the monk's vows, including celibacy. All in all I lived in this situation for nine years. I was an enthusiastic subject in the experiment of bringing Tibetan Buddhism to the West.

On reflection, I was also trying to integrate two different identities that are normally thought of as incompatible or at least conflicting. I wanted to integrate what I believed was the purest form of spiritual practice into a typical Western urban setting. It was my attempt at bridging the East and the West.

While I was a monk I also studied the Tibetan language and the ancient Buddhist texts. In 1983 I gained a Ph.D from the University of Queensland through my examination of Buddhist methods of meditation for realizing egolessness. Throughout these studies I meditated, studied and taught at Buddhist centers. In 1984 I began teaching Asian Philosophy at the university.

After seven years of living life as a domesticated monk, I began to seriously question what I was doing. I recognized that in becoming a monk I had attempted to escape from myself, to be something other than who I was. In assuming the identity of a monk, I strove to be my ideal of a person: calm, insightful, detached and a diligent meditator.

This role also made me different and special in some ways. Yet in doing this I was simply conforming to a model of how I should be, rather than being who I was. Also, in some ways I'd achieved my goal. I'd assimilated and integrated the identities of monk and family man. I was respected in the local and academic communities in which I lived and also by the lamas I knew and the community of Western monks and nuns. I knew how to live the life of monk and family man, and could do this without struggle or discomfort.

Preface

At this point I experienced an identity crisis. My initial intention in becoming a monk had been lost. I had wanted to deeply and experientially connect with concepts like emptiness and non-duality, but I had fallen into a routine, a rut, in having to follow a regimented, daily meditation practice. The spontaneity had gone. My meditation practice was stifling, rather than liberating, me. I felt oppressed rather than freed by my discipline.

I had become habituated to meditation, just like an acceptable drug. I no longer knew who I was. It wasn't at all clear to me even what "being a Buddhist" was.

I began to feel increasingly disconnected from myself yet, paradoxically, more aware of what I was experiencing. Something in me was dying, and at the same time, an awareness was growing. Something was awakening in me that didn't gave a damn about how I felt or what I thought.

For a period of two months I didn't know if I would survive from one day to the next. Nothing I had learned in Buddhism helped me. The different meditative methods I knew did very little or nothing to alleviate the crisis. At times my anxiety and fear were so great that I felt moved to speed up the disintegration of my identity. I felt pushed and pulled between being someone or not existing at all.

As this awakening progressed unrelentingly the *only* thing I could do was to watch it and simply stay aware.

This increasing clarity led me away from the monastic tradition of Buddhism into a Tibetan tradition that is very like Zen. This tradition is called *Dzog Chen* which means "Complete Fulfillment." It is a pristine, non-dogmatic, and expansive form of Buddhism.

The essential teaching of the Complete Fulfillment is that we can be totally and joyfully fulfilled in the moment, independently of our circumstances and conditions, simply by being present and aware. This spoke directly into what I had been experiencing and knew to be true. It was refreshing, revitalizing, simple and powerful.

It now seemed unnecessary to continue being a monk. So I negotiated with my ordaining abbot to give back my vows. I realize now that if I had really understood and assimilated the experience of Complete Fulfillment, I could have remained a monk, since this enables one to release any discomfort and conflict effortlessly, in the moment. Accomplished practitioners of the Complete Fulfillment are, by definition, totally fulfilled wherever and in whatever circumstances they find themselves.

I also see that I connected with the Complete Fulfillment as a "tradition" because I was still seeking some form of "continuity" with my previous involvement in Buddhism. I brought a strategic filter to my understanding of the Complete Fulfillment tradition. I thought I needed to be different if I were to be happy and fulfilled and so I used this newfound tradition to facilitate a change in lifestyle.

As the new phase in my life opened up, many changes were heralded. My marriage was over. It had been damaged beyond repair, especially over the last three or four years of our unusual lifestyle. The constraints of monkhood and behavior appropriate to it were now gone. My affiliations with Buddhist teachers and Buddhist centers slowly fell away and I entered new and unknown territory.

A flood of new feelings, sensations and relationships gradually emerged. Within these a special relationship began to develop with a woman who had had an equally intensive involvement with Buddhism.

Penny's search for meaning and truth had taken her on an interesting journey. Her initial exposure to Buddhism in 1974 led her to travel throughout Asia, studying and practicing different forms of Buddhism. During her stay in Sikkim she fell in love with a Tibetan incarnate lama. After a period of harrowing negotiations with the Tibetan religious authorities, they came to Australia and married. Together they consolidated a Buddhist study and practice center in Melbourne. However, the cultural expectations of Tibetans towards women and the unassailable position of Tibetan lamas within their communities put pressures on their marriage that hadn't been anticipated. The stress of different customs ultimately led to a painful separation. When I met Penny some time later, she was the national organizer for a Buddhist community that was headed up by another Tibetan lama. My overriding impression was of an extremely vital, attractive and spontaneous woman.

From our very first meeting we both had an undeniable sense that our relationship was unavoidable. We also sensed that there was important work to be done in this relationship if we could harness the explosive energy we seemed to catalyze in each other. For me the relationship was the environment, the context for working with the Complete Fulfillment perspective. It was a testing ground for my ability to practice the newfound perspective, since the only approach that worked was to stay with the energy, and be aware and responsive.

With Penny I experienced the same intensity and sheer quantity of energy that I had first encountered on meeting Lama Yeshe. But in this relationship the feelings of security, reliability and dependence that underscored my relationship with Lama Yeshe were entirely absent. Here I had to utilize my own resources to make the relationship work. I was confronted with the energy of Penny's confusion as she rode an emotional rollercoaster for eighteen months. I practiced what I understood Complete Fulfillment to be, and this enabled me—with more or less elegance—to embrace and release the moods and emotions that swirled around me. Eventually clarity and commitment emerged, and we forged a nourishing and fulfilling partnership, a marriage of heart and mind.

During this period we began to explore the best that Western psychology had to offer in terms of personal development. We immersed ourselves in the most innovative and radical technologies that have been developed in the last twenty years. While none of these matched the insights and wisdom of the Buddhist philosophies, they were rich in new methods for transforming our beliefs and emotions. We found their methodologies very interesting, for they enabled many people to have spiritually expanding experiences through fairly short, intensive courses.

In 1986 I was encouraged by Penny and others to design and deliver my own programs. The first of these was called "Therapeutic Applications of Buddhist Psychology." After some time, Penny joined me in delivering the programs we designed as we wove the best of East and West together.

While participants valued our work, we assessed that it was still somewhat fragmented. Somehow it still lacked the essence of what we had learned and experienced. In 1991 I recognized the role of conflicting beliefs in producing stress and saw how this was consistent with the Buddhist Middle Path and the Complete Fulfillment tradition. These and other insights allowed me to synthesize the essence of what I had done, thus producing the backbone of this book. My training in philosophy and Buddhism and more recent immersion in Western technologies fitted together like a perfectly made glove.

I'm now satisfied that I have brought a new measure of coherence and simplicity to many of the esoteric and often complex ideas of Eastern spirituality, psychology and philosophy. Having seen how the jigsaw fits together, we now look forward to sharing this with you.

INTRODUCTION

Over the last thirty years the Western world has witnessed an extraordinary growth of interest in personal development. Each year more and more people are becoming involved in a movement that promises personal growth, greater self-understanding, inner contentment, improved relationships, wealth, health, and so on. Many of us have been active participants in these traditions and programs. Others have been keen observers, waiting for an approach that suits their needs and temperament.

This heartfelt need for a better life has given rise to hundreds of different methods and thousands of courses for improving the quality of our lives. Many people who would not otherwise have been exposed to developing their potential have had opportunities to grow, learn and establish more satisfying lives. On the other hand, the enormous range and sometimes exaggerated promises for happiness and satisfaction have served to perplex and disappoint many. People don't know where to turn next or which advice to take.

What, then, makes this book valuable at a time when dozens of new books appear in the "psychology" and "self-development" sections of bookstores each week? How can we justify yet another?

This book comes at a time when many people are questioning the capacity of existing approaches and techniques to create the real and lasting happiness that they promise. Such questioning isn't hollow since those who are sensing this limitation have often been ardent and committed participants for twenty years or more in the full range of self-development methods.

While the existing paradigm has opened up new possibilities for increased happiness and well-being, it has also rejected other avenues and perspectives that are authentic sources of inner harmony and health.

As a consequence we are now witnessing the emergence of a new approach to well-being, or—as we would have it—the re-discovery of a timeless perspective in a new cultural setting.

Most of the assumptions that underscore the current methodologies for growth and self-development existed prior to the

Western interest in self-development that began some forty years or so ago. They are beliefs that we, as humans, invented thousands of years ago for the purpose of ensuring our survival and well-being. Some of these beliefs are that:

we can control what we experience;

we can choose how we act;

the past affects the present;

our childhood experiences help to shape our personality;

change requires work and application;

the future can be better than the present.

The main contribution of the human potential and self-development movements has been the "empowerment" of these and other beliefs. They have appropriated and then "leveraged" these beliefs in the service of human fulfillment. Thus many of the programs teach us how to "control our thoughts," "manage our lives," "create what we want," "eradicate the negative experiences of childhood," or "replace negative with positive beliefs."

While we don't reject such teachings, we do question the breadth and value of programs that explicitly exclude beliefs which conflict with their own. We question the capacity of these methodologies to thoroughly and comprehensively address the stress and conflict that are so prevalent in our lives.

Since it is these beliefs that are being questioned in a new, emerging paradigm, we will briefly examine the types of blindness that such beliefs can produce. We offer these observations in the spirit of uncovering, and thereby transcending, the limitations of each system of beliefs—just as we encourage others to uncover any blindness in our own work.

The need to control

The need to control our experience is pervasive. There is no arena of our lives that escapes our efforts to influence, manage and control. We attempt to manage our relationships, our careers, our thoughts, our feelings and the physical world. We try to alter our experience with alcohol, drugs, religion, meditation, entertainment, sex and through participating in various courses. We seek to control our staff, our students, and our children. In other relationships we seek control through more "sophisticated" and subtle means. We try to manage our careers by cultivating particular friendships. Perhaps we try to influence our clients or mold public opinion by engaging public relations experts. In overt and covert ways we seek to control our experience and our lives. We continually attempt to modify reality so that it conforms with our ideals and expectations. We cleverly filter out the experiences we want to avoid and contrive to create the ones we desire.

If we have connected with a tradition like Taoism, we might seek to influence our lives by letting go of the need to control every feature and facet of our experience. But even here our "letting go" is for a purpose. "Letting go" is a strategy, a method designed to produce a more mellow and detached outlook on life.

Given this deep seated need to control, it isn't surprising that most of the methodologies we design and use, support this need by teaching "more effective and more powerful" ways to manage and control.

However, the need to constantly organize in the name of creating a workable environment is often tiring and sometimes exhausting. We need to have our hands on the wheel, keeping everything in order and under control, for fear that we might lose our direction and autonomy. Managing, organizing and influencing produces its own stresses and conflicts.

Change for the sake of change?

Another belief that has been cultivated in recent years is that change is valuable in and of itself. Building on a belief that change is inevitable, many methodologies—both old and new—teach that we suffer because we don't accept change. We are told that if we accept change, in ourselves and others, we will be happier. We are taught to accept that "the only constant is change." But then we go further. We are invited to address our fear of change by learning *how* to change. We are encouraged to move "out of the comfort zone." Soon we begin to "embrace" change as a challenge out there for us to overcome. Then we go still further. We start to seek it out. We seek to do what we presently can't do. By now the word "change" has a seductive ring about it. Very soon we are constantly on the look-out for a "major breakthrough" or are trying to find the next experience to knock our socks off. If we aren't growing, if we can't see change in ourselves from one year to the next, we judge ourselves negatively—which just proves to us that we must change.

In the absence of a continual stream of new experiences we can become bored, resigned and frustrated. We can lose our capacity to appreciate the smaller and simpler changes that are always around us in our thoughts and feelings and in the world. The dance of butterflies in the grass or the experience of a gentle breeze on our skin become drowned out by the need for radical stimulation.

Rather than living in true freedom and expansiveness, we live in a state of contraction. Constantly on the look-out for something different, we forever seek to alter our experiences, rather than simply experience them, as they are. And in so doing, we lose our natural ability to be fully present, moment-by-moment, to who we are and what life is.

Instead of becoming free, as we'd initially intended, we just acquire more stories about who we are, where we have been and what we strive for. Our need to be somewhere different from where we are leaves residues of dissatisfaction, tension and over time a feeling of being lost. We become players in an impossible game—telling ourselves that we *can* be complete and perfect, but only if we are someone different from who we are right now.

Yet, many methodologies support this *drive* for change. They promote the transparent belief that fulfillment, peace and harmony depend on changing something. We get trapped in changing just for the sake of change and in so doing we lose sight of what we really want. We create methodologies which suggest that if things were different, if we gained such-and-such new skills, we would be happier. This entire process of believing that we must implement change has become quite transparent. We have reached a point where it is difficult for many people to step outside of these beliefs and freshly ask the questions: "What is the real cause of stress and conflict?" and "How can we live genuinely fulfilled lives?"

The limitation of methods

As previously noted, we automatically try to control our experience in the same way that we drive a car. We try to slow things down when we enjoy what we are doing. We apply the brakes so we can prolong what is pleasurable. When we dislike what is happening to us, we try to speed up and accelerate our way through the experience. We negotiate our way through the detours of our emotions. In order to control the content and intensity of what we are experiencing, we have invented a battery of methods and techniques.

We have methods for suppressing and avoiding emotions we would prefer not to experience (such as fear, vulnerability and anger) and for enhancing emotions we like to experience (such as joy, serenity and confidence). Traditional ways of doing this include ritual dance and music, sex, psychotropic drugs, prayer, yoga exercises and various meditation practices, such as concentrating on the breath or reciting mantras. Contemporary enhancements include affirming beliefs we want to identify with, visualization, ambient music, journaling, catharsis, breathwork and designer drugs. Certainly these methods produce change. Many of them can guarantee rapid and radical changes to our emotions and thoughts.

However, there are limitations in the use of methods that intervene strategically and mechanically with our emotions and thoughts.

As soon as we use a method—any method—there is the question of managing its application. Firstly we need to determine what is the right or best method for us. Then we need to know if we are using it correctly. We must track its application, speculate about its effectiveness and then adjust how and when to use it. We have to practice the method over and over so that it becomes "natural" to remember to use it when necessary. If we use a number of methods from different traditions, we also need to determine if they are compatible with each other. When we rely on methods and strategies for fulfillment, we need to constantly assess where we are and what to do next. Thus, the very methods that are designed to open us to more fulfilling dimensions of existence can have an opposite effect by preoccupying us with the methods themselves.

Also we may fail to see how techniques can condition us so that we have less spontaneity and freedom. To the degree that we adjust our behavior so that it conforms with our chosen set of practices, we condition ourselves in their usage. In time we come to rely and depend on the methods we have learned.

In this way, methods can interfere with the natural and organic evolution of our lives, since they act as filters between what we are experiencing and what we would prefer. Methods and techniques consolidate a division between who we are and what we experience. They can also constrict us by limiting the range of experiences we can accommodate. Certain techniques will block our naked encounters with various emotions. By using them, we may lose our appreciation of the free-flowing and unstructured aspects of life and obscure a more natural source of inner harmony.

The preceding assessments do not reject formal techniques for producing change. They simply note that methods can have both a positive and negative effect on the cultivation of an alert and responsive way of living.

Blinded by our seeking

Many contemporary methodologies foster our need to search for meaning and purpose.

We feel compelled to explain why we are the people we are. We seek causes for our behavior, emotions, strengths, weaknesses and biases. We seek to understand the impact of our childhood, our education, our parents' problems, our past lives and more.

We constantly try to orient ourselves in terms of our past history and expectations for the future. We identify with significant stories about who we are, what we have done and where we think we are going. We offer all sorts of theories and explanations to account for why things are how they are. We search for the deeper meaning behind all that occurs.

We also create meaning and purpose as a carrot to keep us going. We talk about being "on purpose" as though there *is* a right career and true life path for us to discover and tread. We are in a race to discover the real meaning of our lives. Whether we turn inwards as cartographers of inner space or commit ourselves to the creation of an enlightened culture we get seduced by the romantic notions of being seekers, explorers and creators.

If we don't have a new prize to report from our latest adventures we feel small and impoverished. We seek that new program that our friends haven't yet done, a new guru, a new practice, a higher initiation, more peace and more acceptance. Or we might believe we are further along the path and search for the present moment—as if it is something we could find and experience. And if we *try* to be satisfied with what we have already got, instead of achieving happiness, we are left with a residue of resignation.

This search for meaning and fulfillment can disconnect us from the present moment. We find ourselves looking for something that we suspect isn't there, yet we continue to look as though it should be there. This occurs in all areas of our lives. In our close relationships we expect our partners to be always loving, sensitive and caring. In our careers and work we act as though we should be constantly fulfilled and rewarded. We live in the expectation that there must be more than what we presently have.

Yet our seeking for something that isn't there and our expectation that life should be different from what it is, are the very barriers that disconnect us from fulfillment and completion. Blinded by our seeking, we fail to appreciate that we could see what we are looking for if only we stopped looking.

That there is something "to get"

A final assumption that inspires many people to develop their capacities for living fulfilled lives is the belief that fulfillment depends on gaining something. Fulfillment is seen as a function of acquiring some ineffable thing. We may think of this in terms of some knowledge, wisdom, a skill, a capacity, an experience or a way of being. But no matter how we think about it, if we don't gain this experience or understanding, we won't be truly fulfilled. While we sense that this "thing" is elusive and ineffable, we still hold onto the belief that if only we could read the right book, find the right teacher or attend the right course, we would be happy and contented.

Certainly we can and do acquire valuable experiences and skills that help us to manage and cope with the demands of living. But rarely do we question whether or not there is *any* experience or skill that could really fulfil our hopes for peace and contentment. It is unpalatable—even absurd—to think that there is nothing we need to acquire in order to be happy and complete. We reject the possibility that there isn't anything that could finally—once and for all—bring fulfillment. We can't even experiment with an approach to life in which there is nothing *else* we need to get. Instead, we continue to believe that there is some special quality, experience or skill that will fulfil all our needs.

Intrinsic Freedom

The approach described in *Intrinsic Freedom* is significantly different from the methods and techniques we've been exposed to in the past thirty years. One of the main differences is that in *Intrinsic Freedom* we transcend the restriction that we must be different or need to change in order to be fulfilled.

Instead this work is based on the insight that peace and inner harmony arise through our being genuinely open and present to the moment-by-moment flux of our experience. For this insight we are particularly indebted to the Asian cultures which discovered and perfected a range of profound and natural approaches for cultivating a more direct and flexible experience of life.

The essence of the Asian philosophies is the cultivation of wisdom and clarity as distinct from the development of elaborate methods and techniques for changing how we think and act. The approaches that have been taught in philosophies like Taoism and the Complete Fulfillment (*rDzogs chen*) are uncontrived and uncomplicated. Their methods mirror the natural pathways that are traversed whenever we enter a state of real freedom and presence. Consequently, the methods for becoming alert and relaxed recede into the background in exact correspondence with the emergence of heightening presence and awareness. We could say that the procedures and approaches used in these practical philosophies are simply expressions of what *naturally* occurs whenever we authentically resolve stress and conflict, rather than keep it at bay through an act of will-power or suppression.

This book taps the essential wisdom of centuries of practical research into the source of inner contentment and presents it in a framework that is fully accessible to our modern lifestyle and way of thinking.

The book is based on the insight that we experience real freedom when we don't need to avoid what we are experiencing. Whenever we are genuinely present to an experience, without any need to enhance or dilute its quality or texture, we immediately enjoy a unique expansive and liberating way of being. This makes sense, for whenever we need to escape or deny our thoughts, feelings or perceptions we have an experience of being trapped and constrained.

What we call intrinsic freedom stands in marked contrast to conditional forms of freedom. This is the experience of freedom which occurs when life is intermittently consistent with our preferences. This is a limited form of freedom because it depends on our internal and external circumstances matching our desires. Intrinsic freedom, on the other hand, allows us to be free to experience *whatever* life offers us, quite independently of our personal wishes and aspirations.

The experience of intrinsic freedom is also an experience of presence. It is an experience of fully accommodating what is. This is not the same as standing in the face of life's experiences. Rather, it is a totally open and spacious state of being that is, by its very nature, free of stress and conflict. It is a state of full awareness and serenity, where we neither resist our experience nor charge it up. This is a state in which we are aware, relaxed and able to fully embrace all experiences, emotions and thoughts without distortion or the need to escape them.

Intrinsic Freedom describes how we have become disconnected from our source, from many of our feelings, thoughts and beliefs. It tracks the process of how beliefs form in pairs of opposites, separate in order to be distinguished from each other, and ultimately disconnect. It is our conflicting beliefs which are the source of stress and tension.

This book explains how intrinsic freedom is cultivated through harmonizing the specific conflicting beliefs which produce stress and tension. Throughout are exercises which help you to discover which specific beliefs are limiting and stressing you and serving to keep the experience of freedom and presence at a distance. You learn how these limitations and conflicts can easily be harmonized at a foundational level where stress and conflict first originate.

However, learning how to release stress and conflict initially requires controlled conditions and for this reason we have designed an experiential course which is based on the principles and ideas outlined in this book. The structure of this course is described in Appendix Two, pages 129–132.

Natural Release

The practical course introduces an experiential process called Natural Release. This process works within a level of awareness called the Releasing Mind. The Releasing Mind is a foundational level of experience since it is the very source of our beliefs and conflicts.

Natural Release is the approach used by the free-spirited and independent sages who glided through life as carefree and unencumbered individuals. Many of these people were highly public individuals who powerfully influenced the course of history in their roles as politicians, administrators and educators. Enjoying the dynamism and fast-moving pace their positions dictated, they were able to live a stress-free life, experiencing full presence. Others spent their lives in mountain retreats savoring the changing seasons and subtle pleasure and clarity that their meditations produced. Still others lived ordinary family lives, taking on the responsibilities of earning a living and bringing up a family with ease and spontaneity.

Each of us can experience the same level of presence and inner freedom as our notable predecessors. Like them, whether we live in the hurly-burly of city life or in a quiet rural retreat, we too can share a resource that has us fully embracing all that we experience moment by moment. We can live life simply and directly, even in the midst of turmoil and confusion.

As you read this book and do the exercises contained in it, you will discover the real possibility of living with heightened presence and inner harmony. The book will help you recognize what is needed to establish more accepting and loving relationships with yourself and others; and to appreciate a new way to reduce conflict and tension in your life. You begin to sense an innate and ever-present capacity to effortlessly let go of limiting beliefs, thereby living with heightened awareness, alertness and joy.

CHAPTER ONE

What is stress?

One of the symptoms of our competitive, fast-paced society is that we tend to live busy, complex lives where the focus is frequently on results rather than on appreciating the present. Because of this, we tend to live for the future, anticipating and planning what to do next, or get locked into our past, mulling over what's gone wrong.

Our capacity to be fully there—for ourselves, our families, partners and clients—is displaced by a constant need to rectify the past and manage the future. Often we are simply not there to take care of and appreciate the present.

At one level or another we are stressed, feeling pressured by the demands on our time and resources. We feel torn between pursuing different alternatives. Because we commonly link success with stress, we may even believe that we have to be stressed if we are to achieve our goals.

So what is stress? Stress is an experience that everyone recognizes and would generally prefer not to have. Often we talk about our experience of stress by saying that we are "under pressure." We tend to view this pressure as coming from a number of sources. We might believe it is caused by:

other people;

commitments—at work or home;

resources—such as too little or too much money, or too little or too much time, or

physical conditions—such as where we live or our state of health.

When we think about stress it is so easy to focus only on the external circumstances—our work, relationships, children, and so on—but if stress really was caused by something outside us then everyone would have the same reaction to "stressful situations." But we do not. After all, what is highly stressful for one person may induce nothing more than mild frustration in someone else. The same situation might even be stimulating and enjoyable for others. Just think of how differently people relate to events such as speaking in public, getting to work late, or having children. People even respond very differently to illness and physical pain. Clearly, the source of stress lies in our way of thinking.

This is recognized in the new paradigm of health and well-being that is emerging in the West. In this new holistic paradigm, the mind is seen to play a vital role in determining our physical well-being and mental contentment. In the East this has been the dominant way of understanding the human condition for thousands of years. Hinduism, Buddhism and Taoism all teach that the mind is the source of stress and their methods for removing stress all focus on producing changes in attitude and ways of thinking.

In general terms stress is an experience of being in tension. It is a feeling of being pushed, pulled, led, constrained, limited, forced or extended in some way. This feeling of tension or pressure damages us in the same way that receiving a knock to the body causes a bruise or grazing the skin produces an unpleasant sensation.

Much of the time, our daily encounters with the world seem to produce external bruising. We experience nearly constant friction between ourselves and the world as we brush up against circumstances, people and situations that we would prefer not to have to deal with. Often we are so habituated to this experience that we barely notice it, yet it continues to affect us. Only when it is of major significance and very stressful do we give it our attention.

In addition to this external bruising is the internal bruising that we mete out to ourselves in the form of judgments and expectations. No wonder by the end of a day we often need to recover—in preparation for tomorrow's encounter with ourselves and the world.

This familiar and pervasive experience of stress is discussed and directly addressed in this book and in the accompanying practical course. The course guides you into an experience of stress-free awareness and teaches you how to create this easily for yourself.

Definition of stress

We define stress as any experience that we believe could or should be different from what it is.

This is a very comprehensive understanding of stress. Its particular strength is that it allows us to address all forms of stress, from the most intense through to the most subtle.

Intense stress

Our understanding of stress includes intensely distressing experiences that can occur in the breakdown of relationships, traumatic injury or illness, career crises, the loss of a loved one and our own death. It also includes the stress that often surrounds events such as pregnancy, childbirth, retirement, or entering an intimate relationship.

The stress of daily life

Our definition also covers the stresses of daily existence. These include such things as having to manage our work, our finances, our education, health and relationships. Also included is the stress of having to deal with an uncertain future. Sometimes just thinking about these necessities can be distressing.

Annoying experiences

Our definition also includes the less stressful, though annoying, experiences that regularly seem to happen to us—daily. Thus, we include the stress and tension that can arise from events such as wasting time in a meeting, burning the dinner, not finding the shoes we are shopping for or locking our keys in the car.

Our understanding of stress also allows us to detect the subtle stresses that pervade most of our lives: anticipating the end of a pleasant experience, pleasures lost through having to sleep, simply knowing that our bodies are prone to illness and pain and having to take care of them accordingly.

Subtle stress

Our definition also lets us recognize the most subtle forms of stress that occur even in our most sublime experiences. From our point of view, even the experiences in which we say: "Wow! This is wonderful. How can it be so good? Do I really deserve this?" have an element of stress in them. Why? Because very often we do not fully accept the joy (and graciousness) of the experience itself. Frequently we question and doubt even our most precious experiences. Even in the midst of a positive experience of love, joy or serenity, we may think "Will this last? I hope I don't lose this. What do I have to do to make sure it won't go away? How do I get it back if it stops?" We actually introduce stress by interfering with the organic flow of the experience.

Subtle stresses can function in the same way as a tiny stress fracture in an airplane. At the beginning they can't be detected, but they can grow and, in extreme cases, cause an accident. Subtle stresses can seed the destruction of a pleasant experience. We talk ourselves out of the experience by thinking: "Will this last?" "Do I deserve it?" and the like. Within minutes or even seconds a thoroughly enjoyable experience can become diluted and degraded into a fading memory.

SUMMARY

Stress is any experience we have which we judge could or should be different from what it is.

Experiences are stressful because we do not fully and unconditionally accept them.

The signs of stress

Many of the signs of stressful living are familiar to us since stress affects all aspects of our well-being. Stress affects us physically, emotionally and mentally. It reduces our capacity for effective work and hinders our ability to establish fulfilling and loving relationships.

Damage to our physical health

The effects of stress on our physical health are well known. It is now widely acknowledged by the medical sciences that illnesses and diseases such as migraine, asthma, allergies, hypertension, heart disease and cancer can be caused or aggravated by stressful living. It is well documented that long-term stress reduces the body's resistance to viruses and infections and healing is retarded by a stressful lifestyle.

Habits and social problems

Stress is a major contributing factor to addictions to substances such as alcohol, tobacco and prescription and illicit drugs. Social problems such as violence in the home, child abuse, rape, homicide and suicide are also closely related to stress.

A range of psychosomatic and psychological problems are also connected to stress. These include for example, insomnia, hypermotility (the inability to stay still), headaches, sexual difficulties and eating disorders such as anorexia and bulimia.

Exaggerated behaviors

Other more general conditions that signal the presence of stress are fatigue, undue seriousness, defensiveness, belligerence, irritability, frustration, worry, nervousness, crying, tenseness, preoccupation, impulsive behavior, and difficulty in concentrating. Exaggerated emotions such as rage, anger, sadness and depression are also signs of internal stress and conflict.

Moodiness

The moods that seem to be so much a part of our times, such as anxiety, loneliness, resentment and resignation are all conditions of stress. In every case in which someone experiences, say anxiety, boredom or resentment, they are judging that things could or should be different from what they are. For example, if we are bored we believe that something should be happening now that isn't happening. Perhaps we should be having fun, mixing with other people rather than sitting at home by ourselves. If we are resentful, we are judging that someone has done something to us that they shouldn't have done.

Signs of stress-free living

Some of the signs of being free of stress are that we are calm, contented, relaxed, joyful, invigorated and peaceful. When we are totally enjoying an experience, with no preoccupying or nagging doubts, when we are simply being present to our experiences, then we can say we are free of stress. If we find that we are not calm, invigorated and so on, we can conclude that we are in a state of tension to a greater or lesser degree.

CHAPTER TWO

The source of stress

Stress occurs when we believe that things could or should be different from how they are; that is, stress is caused by a differential between "how things are" and "how we would like them to be."

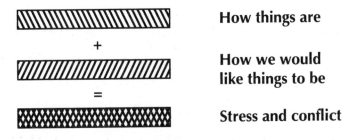

How things are

+

How we would like things to be

=

Stress and conflict

The source of stress

How often do we have "if only" thoughts? Take some of these familiar examples: "If only I had more time . . .," "If only I had more money . . . ," "If only I didn't have to . . .," "If only I could . . .," "If only I were like . . . ." These examples demonstrate how familiar and ever-present stress is in our lives. You could compile your own extensive list of "if only's." These stresses, which vary from mild to severe, seem to accompany a good deal of our waking lives.

The level of stress we experience is a function of two factors: (1) the degree of difference between "how things are" and "how we would like them to be" and (2) the significance or importance of that difference for us. The greater the difference, the more intense the stress. The more significant the difference, the greater the stress. The following table helps to show this.

Degree of difference	Significance	Levels of stress
Small	Not important	Minimum stress
Large	Not important	Min-med stress
Small	Important	Min-med stress
Large	Important	Medium stress
Small	Very important	Medium stress
Large	Very important	Maximum stress

EXERCISE

Take two or three stressful experiences. Firstly, describe each experience in general terms. Then describe each experience in terms of (1) the difference between "how things were" and "how you would have liked them to be" and (2) how important or significant the difference was (or wasn't) for you.

EXAMPLE ONE

The experience: *I felt upset and was unable to sleep well for more than a week after failing a final exam.*

How it was: *I failed and didn't graduate.*

How it should have been: *I should have passed because I did all the work and studied very hard.*

The difference: *It is the difference between passing and failing.*

The importance: *This was very important to me because without graduating I will have to do another whole year's work.*

Result: *Medium to maximum stress.*

EXAMPLE TWO

The experience: *I forgot that I had a meeting, realised only 15 minutes before it was due to start and I was late.*

How it was: *I was 10 minutes late.*

How it should have been: *I shouldn't have forgotten, shouldn't have had to rush and I should have been on time.*

The difference: *It is the difference between being on time and a little late.*

The importance: *This was not that important, particularly as others arrived after me.*

Result: *Minimum stress.*

EXAMPLE THREE

The experience: *I feel totally worn out because I have to get up several times each night to attend to my baby.*

How it is: *I am sleeping about four hours a night and I'm unable to concentrate during the day.*

How it should be: *I should be sleeping properly. My baby should be sleeping right through the night. Other babies her age do. I should be alert during the day.*

The difference: *It is the difference between sufficient and insufficient sleep.*

The importance: *Very important because I have to go to work each day and can't function properly.*

The difference: *Medium to maximum stress function.*

If we are to understand the secret of stress-free living, we need to look at the relationship between "how things are" and "how things should be" more closely. When we say that there is conflict between "how things are" and "how we would like them to be," we need to determine what this conflict is about. If stress is a tension within something, what is it that is in tension? In other words, what is the medium within which conflict occurs?

Our preferences are beliefs

When we think to ourselves or describe to others "how we would like things to be," what we are doing is formulating a preference—and in so doing we are formulating our beliefs. We believe that circumstances should be like such-and-such or that things could be different. We think that it could have been like this or that, rather than how it is. What we are expressing therefore are our beliefs or interpretations. Otherwise people couldn't agree or disagree about "how things should be."

Our experience of "how things are" depends on beliefs

When we think about "how things are," we tend to believe that this is independent of our preferences, wishes, beliefs or interpretations. We believe that our experience of "how things are" has nothing or very little to do with our beliefs, opinions or judgments.

A belief is a mechanism for generating experience

However, this is not the case. To have a belief is not just to have a vague opinion about something. A belief is a mechanism for generating our experience. For example, if I believe that "I'm a tidy person," then I don't see the mess that others—who believe that I am untidy—will see. For me, there actually is no mess. It doesn't exist.

Even if we take a very concrete experience, such as sitting here reading this, we cannot understand it, we cannot experience it independently of a whole set of transparent beliefs about such things as what we are, what reading is, what sitting is, what we are reading, the meaningfulness of what is read and so on. Said simply, our experience is filtered and shaped by our beliefs. For example, the flower arrangement opposite will be seen quite differently by different people. For some it will be an organic sculpture. For others it will be a flower arrangement. For someone who is skilled in the Japanese art of ikebana, it will have an aesthetic dimension and subtlety that evades other observers.

BELIEF FILTERS

Our experience is filtered by beliefs

A lot of research has been done on how language and conceptuality shape perception. It is well known that the Eskimos have more than twenty names for what we call snow. The point is that because of the fine linguistic distinctions they have made, they actually see the landscape differently. Where we would see just a white carpet of snow, Eskimos see a richly varied tapestry of color, texture, sheen and other subtleties.

In the absence of a concept we can't have an experience of what the concept points to. When Tibetans saw airplanes for the first time during the Chinese invasion of Tibet in the 1950s, they didn't know what they were. They hadn't been prepared for the phenomenon as we had through the drawings of Leonardo da Vinci and the various experimental prototypes that preceded the real thing. Consequently, when the Tibetans looked into the sky, they had no idea that the fighter planes were large, piloted, mechanically driven machines of destruction. They had to invent a word for airplane and the word they invented clearly indicates how primitive their first perceptions were. The word they invented was "nam dru" *(gnam gru)* which means sky boat. Their word for airport is "nam dru bab tung" *(gnam gru'i babs thang)* which literally means "a landing plain for sky boats." (Tibet is land-locked and doesn't have ports.)

This same phenomenon occurs whenever we see something completely new. We can only see it through our familiar concepts and ideas. The picture below is an early Australian Aboriginal drawing of European explorers riding pack-horses. The horses have large hind legs and long tails. Their front legs are much smaller, like paws. When the first Aborigines sighted horses, they looked to them like kangaroos. Similarly, the first paintings of kangaroos done by Europeans always showed them with their front paws on the ground and small tails.

The first Aboriginal sighting of Europeans on horseback

When we talk about "how things are," we do so as an expression of our beliefs. Whenever we say: "Things are like this," we have a belief that: "This is how things are." For example, when someone asks us: "How are things going?"—we reply by offering our beliefs about how things are. We might say that everything is great or that everything is going wrong. We might say that we just sold our house or that we've just begun a new job. All of these are beliefs.

EXERCISE

Try to describe "how things are" or what is happening for you right now without relying on any beliefs.

Stress is caused by conflicting beliefs

Both "how things are" and "how we would like things to be" are beliefs. They are complex sets of beliefs. When we feel stressed, our beliefs are in tension or conflict with each other. Stress is actually caused by a conflict in our beliefs, rather than a conflict between reality and what we believe.

In fact, it isn't possible to be in conflict with reality. Reality just is. It isn't this way or that way. It isn't good or bad, desirable or undesirable. We can't object to it or approve of it because, outside of our beliefs, it just is.

It is only our beliefs about reality that can conflict. This is why experiencing reality or "being real" automatically releases all conflict.

EXERCISE

1   *Recall a recently stressful experience. Experience the belief that the situation, event or feeling shouldn't have been as it was. How does this feel?*
2   *Now replace that belief with the belief "that it can only be as it is." Now experience that. How does it feel?*

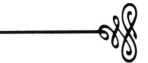

CHAPTER THREE

Beliefs

What are beliefs?

So far we have discovered that stress is created by conflicting beliefs. In order to determine how we create stress through conflicting beliefs, we need to understand what beliefs are.

Beliefs represent what is

A belief is a representation. We can experience what a belief represents, but we cannot say what a belief represents since it is only the belief that tells us what it represents. The things that beliefs represent don't have the capacity to tell us what they are. They just are. It is the function of beliefs to represent what is. When we believe that our representations *are* what they represent we cannot experience things as they are. So, for the most part, our beliefs disconnect us from reality.

The very origins of the verb "to believe" indicate this disconnection. The word comes from Old English and Old High German roots that mean "to hold dear" or "cherish" and "to make palpable or acceptable to oneself." The traditional meaning has nothing to do with what is true or real. It is closer to what we call an opinion.

QUERY
Does this mean we have to get rid of all beliefs if we are to experience things as they are?

ANSWER
Not at all. All we need to do is to experience our beliefs as they are. We need to experience our beliefs as beliefs—as representations of things that we cannot know except as representations. We can experience the primitive energy or form that they are. As with other things, we can experience the 'isness' of our beliefs.

In the practical course, your beliefs will change and evolve in a way that is appropriate for you. You continue to entertain beliefs, but they are for the pure sake of entertainment. They become fluid and flowing rather than rigid, conflicting and deeply entrenched. Your beliefs begin to manifest as the free play of an inner world.

There are different types of beliefs. Some are simple and others are complicated collections of simpler beliefs. For example, there are:

identifications
characterizations
judgments
opinions
interpretations
explanations
theories.

Identifications are the simplest beliefs. Theories are the most complex.

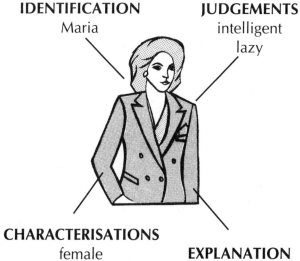

IDENTIFICATION
Maria

JUDGEMENTS
intelligent
lazy

CHARACTERISATIONS
female
married
teacher
Brazilian

EXPLANATION
Maria is intelligent
because her parents
were both doctors

Types of beliefs

The form of beliefs

We distinguish beliefs on the basis of their form or structure.

EXERCISE

How could you distinguish one belief from another if they were formless?

Note *It will not work to say that it is the experience to which a belief refers that distinguishes one belief from another. For if this were the case, then any belief could represent any experience.*

Some philosophers have said that beliefs have the structure of propositions, but this is only part of the story.

Beliefs also have a form. We are not usually aware of the form of beliefs because their form is more subtle and intangible than the shapes and forms of physical objects. However, our moods and emotions provide a window on the shape and form of beliefs. We need only reflect on how we speak about our moods and emotions to see this. The way we speak about our moods and emotions suggests the form of our beliefs.

The shape of our moods and emotions

A depressed mood, for example, is often thought of as dark, solid, heavy, thick and sluggish. An excited mood can move unpredictably, in jerks and starts, swirling and spiky like a bubbling brook or fast-moving stream. A mood of peace has a form of continuity, smoothness, expansiveness and uniformity. Moods are also associated with colors. Anger, for example, is often thought of as red; jealousy as green; and serenity as pastel colors such as mauve and soft blue. Fear is depicted as black or dark grey.

These descriptions are not mere metaphors since colors can help to evoke the experiences. They are clues to the internal structure and shape of our beliefs. One of the skills of award-winning novelists is their ability to sense and describe the form and structure of human moods and emotions.

EXERCISE 1

Close your eyes and recall a specific time when you were experiencing an intense mood or emotion such as anger, excitement, depression. Now re-live it. Experience it as though it were happening to you now. Begin to notice its shape, its texture, dimensions, consistency. Does it have a boundary? Is it dense or light? Does it have an energy? For example, is it dynamic, static or poised? Does it have a color, etc? How does this alter your perception of space and time? Now gently bring your attention back to where you are right now.

EXERCISE 2

Let us go into this further. In particular, let's see if we can deepen our experience of how beliefs influence our experience.

1. *Focus your awareness on a single object. It could be something in this room, a sound you can hear or an image of something you are familiar with, for example, something in your own home. Narrow your attention to simply that object.*

2. *Now allow your awareness to expand to include everything in the room. Now go beyond this and expand your awareness to include everything outside of this room as well. Expand your awareness to include everything that exists in and beyond this universe.*

3. *Focus your attention on the present moment. Exclude from your awareness all memories of the past and thoughts of the future. Direct your attention just to this moment.*

4. *Now expand your awareness to include all past memories right back to your earliest years and beyond. Now expand your awareness to include all thoughts of the future, including your own death, and beyond this as far as you can imagine—even beyond the end of this solar system.*

Now gently bring your attention back to where you are right now.

REFLECT

Were these experiences the same or different? What might account for any difference?

Moods and emotions are shaped by beliefs

Moods and emotions have different forms and in order to complete the picture, we need to see how they relate to beliefs. What is the connection between our moods and emotions and our beliefs? Moods are created by quite specific beliefs; so we can begin to see through our moods how beliefs have different forms.

Moods and emotions are functions of our beliefs about the past and the future. These two sets of beliefs come together and produce the emotions and moods we experience at any point in time.

Beliefs about the past — Memories → **MOODS EMOTIONS** ← **Beliefs about the future** — Anticipation

For example, if we believe that our circumstances are hopeless and we can't see this changing in the future, we will very likely feel miserable and resigned.

On the other hand, if we believe we will be able to act competently and effectively in the future, we will feel confident and composed.

QUERY

If beliefs have a form then where do they exist? Can we locate them?

ANSWER

Yes, we can. They are where we experience them. And in this they are no different from physical forms. Everything is located where you experience it.

In reality there is no north, south, east or west, no up or down, no front or behind, no inside or outside. These are all judgments and interpretations. The most we can say is that we find things where we find them. Where that is we cannot say unless we refer to a belief or interpretation.

If we want, we can begin to locate beliefs in the same way that we locate physical objects.

Levels of belief

There are two ways in which beliefs can conflict. Sometimes when we get stressed it is easy to see what is causing the stress. For example, if we are in a traffic jam en route to an appointment, the stress we experience is caused by beliefs such as: "I will get there on time," "No, I won't get there on time," "It will matter if I am late," "No, it won't matter if I am late." This type of stress is caused by "conflicts between our surface beliefs." It is easy to appreciate these beliefs because they are quite accessible to us. They are expressed in our thinking which we can easily become aware of. In fact, thoughts are an expression of our surface beliefs.

However, other stresses we experience are caused by conflicts between our surface beliefs and beliefs that lie deeper in our thoughts and personality. We call these "deep" or "transparent beliefs." Because we are often not aware of our deep beliefs, we may not be aware of this source of stress.

SURFACE BELIEFS

► STRESS ◄   ► STRESS ◄

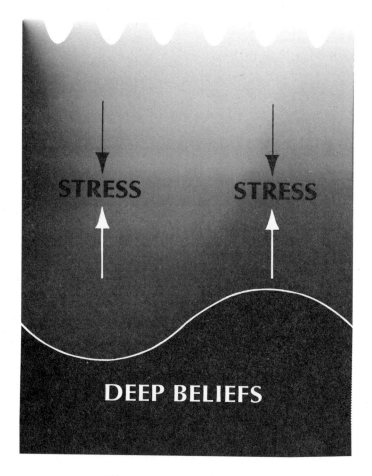

STRESS   STRESS

DEEP BELIEFS

The source of stress

Deep beliefs

A deep belief is one that gives foundational structure to our experience of ourselves and the world. Deep beliefs set up our basic orientation to ourselves and the world. Examples of these beliefs are: "I can't succeed," "I can succeed," "I'm not smart enough," "The world is full of opportunities," "People can't be trusted."

Essentially, any belief can be a deep belief. What makes it a deep belief is the fact that the belief is always in the background shaping our experiences of and responses to the world. And because they act in the background, deep beliefs are often very transparent. In a sense we can't see them. They are so close to us that we are inside them.

Deep beliefs are the ones that really grab us. They are the beliefs that have so much grip on who we are and how we live our lives that we usually fail to see them as beliefs. They stick so closely to us that we constantly overlook them. The ones that are most obvious are the ones we are most blind to. Their closeness makes them invisible. In just the same way that fish cannot see the water they swim in—so we are blind to many of the beliefs that shape our lives. Our deep beliefs are like water to fish—they are the environment, the context of our lives. We are in them, quite literally, and being in them we can't see them.

We take it for granted that we are real and separate from others, that there is a world "out there" for us to experience, and that it is physical and solid. These are "givens." Such experiences are so much a part of our existence that we no longer see them as reflections of our foundational or constituting beliefs.

Our beliefs are like our eyes. We see with and through our beliefs. Just as we are not aware of our own eyes when we see, similarly we are not aware of our beliefs shaping our experience. We just experience.

Experiencing our deep beliefs

In order to remove stress and conflict from our lives, we need to appreciate the deep beliefs that structure our lives, since most pervasive and constant forms of stress are caused by conflicts between our surface and our deep beliefs.

So how can we experience our deep beliefs if they are hidden from our immediate attention?

Our deep beliefs show up in the recurrent patterns in our lives. We experience the world as a reflection of our deep beliefs.

Our battles in and with the world are reflections of the internal conflicts in our beliefs.

If we are lonely and feel isolated, then we probably have a number of deep beliefs about people being untrustworthy, that we are unlovable, that it is best to be self-reliant, etc. If we find that we are always being taken for granted, this may reflect a deep belief that we don't deserve recognition or thanks.

We can discover our deep beliefs by being honest and open to ourselves about how we feel and respond to the world. If we struggle with the idea that it could be easy to discover our deep beliefs then we have just uncovered a deep belief—that it is difficult to really get to the source of what causes our problems. It is this sort of belief that leads people to engage in long-term therapy, to struggle with a spiritual discipline or to enrol in one cathartic workshop after another.

Though our deep beliefs are invisible to us, with training we can discover them in just the same way the master mariners of old, such as the Polynesians, could sometimes detect unseen land masses and islands over the horizon by observing the interference patterns on the surface movements of the ocean.

Conflicts between surface and deep beliefs

Sometimes our surface beliefs and our deep beliefs correspond with each other. For example, it is a surface and a deep belief that we exist. Similarly, the belief in gravity exists at both a surface and deep level.

At other times our surface beliefs are inconsistent with our deep beliefs. We may say that we love someone when deep down we are indifferent to them, or even dislike them. And conversely, we might say that we loathe someone but underneath this we have a deep affection for them. Or we might believe that we aren't frightened of authorities, but deep down we are terrified. We might say that we dislike our work, yet deep down it is satisfying. That is to say, it satisfies all our needs about what we believe we deserve.

Surface Belief What you say you believe, or think you believe.
Deep Belief   What you really believe.

We may not believe what we think we believe

Since our beliefs can be inconsistent in this way, it follows that
sometimes we tell ourselves something is true when this is *not*
what we really believe. At other times, we honestly believe that
what we tell ourselves is *not* true. The reason we do this is that
we don't want to acknowledge some things which are true for
us. Really we are kidding ourselves about what we believe. The
types of beliefs that fit into this category are:

I enjoy physical pain;
I am selfish;
I don't want to be happy;
I don't want to be responsible.

If you dismiss these as possibilities, if you find it incredible that
you really could believe that you don't want to be happy, that
you enjoy physical pain, or don't love your spouse, parents or
children, you should ask: "Why do I attract pain, suffering,
loneliness, or whatever into my life?"

EXERCISE

1   *How can you discover what your deep beliefs are?*
2   *What are your deep beliefs?*

Sometimes our conflicting beliefs are not obvious

The conflicting beliefs underscoring our stress and tension are
obscured by the stories we create in order to explain why we
feel pressured or strung out. In these explanations we usually
recognize only one side of what we are thinking and feeling.

Take the situation where we are feeling stressed at work. The explanation that we usually offer might run along the lines that we can't stand our work. There is too much to do, our boss is unsympathetic to our needs, we don't have enough support staff . . . All up, we say we can't cope. However, we do go to work each day, and in general terms we get our work done. So to the extent that we continue in our work, we can stand it and we do cope. Our stress is caused by the conflicting beliefs that we can and cannot cope with our work responsibilities. If we truly couldn't stand it, if we really couldn't cope, we would be somewhere else, doing some other type of work.

This blindness to the conflicting beliefs that produce stress and conflict is also common in dysfunctional relationships. How often have we all heard the stories of people who are in painful and limiting relationships? We may have been in them ourselves, complaining about what he or she does; saying that our partner is selfish, inconsiderate, that it will never improve and that we want it to end. We do believe these things. But if this were *all* we believed then the relationship would end. However, we also believe that it might improve and that we shouldn't get out. So ultimately the stress and conflict are caused by our own conflicting beliefs—beliefs that it will improve and that it won't improve, that we should leave and that we shouldn't leave.

Even the uncomfortable feeling, say, of needing a cigarette can be tracked in this way. On the one hand we believe that we can't wait any longer for a cigarette. But on the other hand, if we are still waiting, then clearly we also believe that we *can* wait. The uncomfortable feeling arises because we are sitting between two conflicting beliefs—that we can't wait and that we can wait.

Conflicting beliefs can be tracked in this way for all the situations in which people are stressed or under pressure.

EXERCISE

Recall a recent (or recurring) situation in which you felt in conflict or stress. Recall what happened and as you do this, begin to identify the beliefs you were oscillating between.

Now observe the situation again, with awareness of these conflicting beliefs. Does the situation appear any different? Do you feel any differently about it now?

CHAPTER FOUR

Why do our beliefs conflict?

Knowing that stress is caused by conflicting beliefs, you might ask if our beliefs must conflict with each other. In order to answer this, it's necessary to examine how beliefs form.

All our beliefs form in pairs of opposites because concepts, which are the building blocks of our beliefs, are defined by their opposites.

First recognized by the ancient Chinese sages thousands of years ago, this insight is the basis of Taoism and the meaning of the yin-yang symbol.

As Lao Tsu writes in the *Tao Te Ching*:

When all the world knows beauty, there is ugliness.
When they know good as good there is evil.
In this way existence and non-existence produce each other.
Difficult and easy complete each other.
Long and short contrast each other.
Pitch and tone harmonize each other.
Future and past follow each other.

The concept "tall," for example, is only meaningful to us because we contrast it with "short." If we didn't have the concept "short," then "tall" would be a totally meaningless word. Similarly, the concept of "self" depends on the concept "other"; "wealth" on "poverty"; "love" on "hatred"; and so on. Without the contrast, a concept has no meaning.

Beliefs form in pairs of opposites

For every belief we have, we also have an opposite belief. Perhaps we don't believe that we have such a belief, but we do. Why? Because the meaning or reference of every belief depends on an opposite belief.

Because the two opposites are inseparable, we can talk about a unit of belief. A unit of belief consists of two fragments—concept A and its opposite, not A. Together they are a unit.

EXERCISE

Take any concept—for example, fire, house, coffee, fear— and try to define it without referring to anything that it isn't.

QUERY

Why can't we make all our beliefs consistent with each other so that they no longer conflict? Can't we create only one type of belief, the sort that forms a coherent and stable picture of who we are and the world we live in? For example, I can try to always and only believe the same things about myself. I might try to believe only that I am intelligent, caring and attractive and never think that I am dumb, selfish or ugly, no matter what the circumstances or what I am experiencing.

ANSWER

If you have tried to do this, then like many others, you will have found it impossible, for we cannot always think consistently, without any doubts, conflicts or contradictions. This is no reflection whatsoever on our thinking skills, our commitment or our mental power. It is impossible to think consistently. However, up to this point in our lives, this is one of the major ways in which we have attempted to remove stress and conflict. We have tried to change our beliefs so that we only believe the things we want to believe about ourselves and others.

How do beliefs form?

Understanding how beliefs form in the first place, we can better appreciate how beliefs conflict with each other.

An important insight of the Oriental sages was that beliefs co-exist in pairs of opposites. This is also how beliefs form in the first place. They form in pairs that contradict each other. Two opposite beliefs co-emerge. The following diagram illustrates how beliefs co-emerge, become separate and finally dis-connect from each other. Initially the two opposite beliefs co-exist. Then in order to establish fixed positions and definite opinions about ourselves and the world and give things distinct and permanent characteristics, we push the two beliefs apart and suppress one belief from our awareness.

In fact, every time we assert or deny a particular belief—every time we think: "This is such-and-such,"—we simultaneously dis-connect an opposite belief. Beliefs become solid and real for us to the extent that the opposite beliefs become transparent.

In the process of formation a belief divides into two fragments or opposites. The two fragments depend on each other for their existence, yet at the same time they threaten each other's existence.

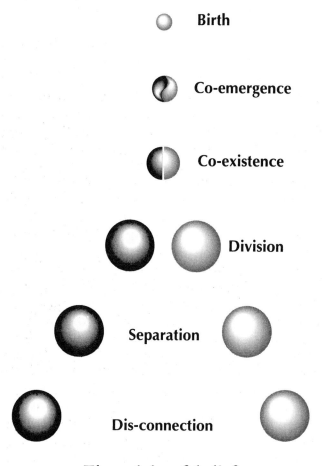

Birth

Co-emergence

Co-existence

Division

Separation

Dis-connection

The origin of beliefs

EXERCISE

You might like to consider what triggers the birth of a belief.

How WE come into existence

The most significant belief for each of us is a belief in our own existence. It is also significant that we each have our own identity. It is important that we are different since if we aren't different we don't exist. Together, these beliefs—that we are and that we have such-and-such an identity—produce who we are. These beliefs create the person we are. They give us our sense of separateness from others and the world we live in. Also they give us the personality characteristics and history we have.

Because we are our beliefs about who we are, we come into existence in just the same way that all beliefs come into existence. First we develop the belief in a self (or me) through contrast with "the other" (or not me). Having created the belief in a self, we then attribute characteristics to it. We build up an identity by building up a set of beliefs, for example, that we are vulnerable, sexy, funny, intelligent or lazy.

Each time we attribute a characteristic to ourselves through holding a belief, we split the opposite characteristic off and hold it at a distance. We push it away. One way we often do this is by attributing an opposite characteristic to others. We project the characteristic we don't want to have onto others. We say that we are selfless and others are selfish. Or we call ourselves hardworking and others lazy. While holding one set of beliefs close to our heart (owning them, possessing them and identifying with them) we push the opposing characteristics away. We dis-identify with them. The following diagram shows how this happens.

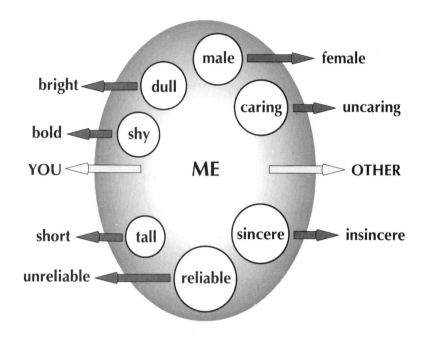

Forming an identity

The stress of physical pain

Physical pain is one of the most overt sources of stress, yet the real source of stress lies not in the pain itself but in a dilemma about how we relate to it.

When we experience physical pain, the pain or discomfort is a fact, so something tells us that we must accept it. Yet on the other hand, we reject the painful experience. We try to suppress it or think it out of existence. We get tied up inside a conversation about whether we can stand the pain or not. We become immersed in making decisions about whether we should seek medical attention or whether we should take painkillers, about whether or not our condition is serious.

The stress that accompanies physical pain centers around the conflicting beliefs that "I can stand the pain . . ." and "I cannot stand the pain." Oscillating between these thoughts results in increasingly intense stress.

In an effort to resolve this conflict, we may try to give in to our belief that "I can't stand the pain." But even though we give up and admit that we just can't stand it, still we continue to bear the pain, second after second, minute after minute. Our strategy for relieving the pain by "giving into it" doesn't work. Our pain still persists. So our beliefs about whether or not we can stand pain continue to conflict.

Alternatively, we may try to alleviate our stress by telling ourselves that we can stand our pain. This is the heroic approach—put on a stoic face, grit our teeth, and struggle to suppress a physical pain. Or perhaps we become a martyr and attempt to tolerate the pain by convincing ourselves that it is good for us. However, such approaches invariably create their own stress since we are rejecting the belief that we "can't stand the pain." We don't accept that we "can't tolerate our pain and discomfort."

The stress of dis-connection

The state of dis-connection is unnatural and inherently stressful because it involves pushing beliefs apart and holding them separate in order to maintain a set of fixed views and opinions about ourselves and the world. Dis-connection is a contrived and artificial state sustained through constant work and enormous effort. For each belief, there is an opposite belief which can be viewed as a threat. Consequently, there is a whole set of beliefs that we try to exclude from our thinking and feeling. We push these beliefs away and hold them as far away as we can. Because we fear letting down our defenses, we actively reject all beliefs that threaten our view of the world.

Pushing threatening beliefs away

However, if we begin to let go of this effort, even for a minute, and allow ourselves to experience the initial fear that might occur, we begin to experience a state of peace and calm. If we allow ourselves to go further with this feeling, it very quickly transforms into an experience of uplifting and totally aware serenity.

How do beliefs imply their opposite?

Once our beliefs are dis-connected from each other, naturally it is difficult to see how they are connected. The nature of dis-connection is to disguise the interdependence of beliefs and feelings. Sometimes we consciously resist seeing the connection between opposite beliefs. In fact, the more dis-connected beliefs are, the more difficult it is to appreciate how each belief implies an opposite belief. Since in our ordinary state of consciousness most of our beliefs are dis-connected, we cannot expect to recognize an opposite belief for every belief we observe.

However, as we become sensitive to the nature of beliefs, we can begin to see how every belief expresses an opposite belief. Indeed, it becomes apparent that everything we do or say expresses its opposite, and apparent pairs of opposites co-exist.

While our beliefs always express an opposite belief and our actions and feelings have two aspects to them, this should not be confused with the simple, unconfused and uncomplicated process of experiencing the natural flow of thoughts and feelings that we have each day. What is meant here is the way we interrupt or interfere with the organic flow and unfolding of life by trying to grab on to or reject what we are feeling and thinking. This is how we get stuck, bogged down in the flow of life.

There are many ways we do this. We may need to know what we are feeling or we may want to control our thoughts and feelings. On some occasions we try to slow time down by applying the brakes, perhaps through fear of what might come next or to savor a particular experience.

At other times we try to push our way through an experience in anticipation of something better or because we judge that it is unpleasant or painful. At these times our experience becomes frozen in one way or another—and our emotions and moods become an expression of conflicting beliefs.

Yet when we accept and appreciate our experience, our emotions and moods unfold gently and effortlessly in their own time and manner.

Although it is difficult to observe how beliefs imply an opposite belief when we are dis-connected, it is possible to gain a glimpse of how beliefs co-exist by observing the emotional paradoxes that occur in daily life. A few examples may help to stimulate your own observations.

Pleasure and pain

We often experience the two-sided nature of emotions at the transition points in our lifetimes, for these are the points at which we have not yet consolidated an emotional style. For example, at the beginning and end of close relationships we often experience emotional paradoxes. We may find that the pleasure of being with someone is also painful. It hurts to be so fulfilled by someone else. The feelings can be so fresh and intense that it's hard to say what we are feeling. It is only as the relationship becomes a "known quantity" that our emotions become solid and well-defined.

Underneath our automatic response to pain is the pleasure we gain from our sorrows and difficulties. Often we soak in our pain just as we might enjoy a hot bath. Becoming self-absorbed in the stories we tell ourselves about our predicament, we enjoy attending to our pain and sorrow by sharing it with others, reminiscing about the difficulties of life or praising ourselves for our capacity to endure misery and disappointment.

Conviction and doubt

One example that may be familiar is when someone expresses doubt when they voice their certainty. When someone says: "I am completely convinced of such-and-such," you can often also hear uncertainty. It is as though the expression of conviction simultaneously triggers an expression of doubt. It even seems that saying: "I am convinced" is somehow an expression of doubt.

Boredom and inspiration

Initially it sounds unlikely, but boredom makes us alive. There is a slight rush of energy and invigoration that comes when we openly acknowledge that we are flat or bored. Really feeling our boredom can be a source of invigoration. Finally we get so bored that we are actually inspired—inspired to do something different. At first it may sound odd, but when you examine the experience itself, intense boredom (as opposed to "turning off") is a very invigorated state.

Indifference and love

When we assert: "I love so-and-so" or "I love you," there can also be an expression that love is missing. When we express our love towards someone we simultaneously express that we don't love them—otherwise we would not find ourselves communicating our belief about our love. Love would just be there. Our assertions of love are an expression that what we say is there is actually missing. When we say: "I love you," we may also be saying: "I don't love you."

Accepting and rejecting

We create stress each time we wish that something was different from how it is. Every time we reject or resist a situation we find ourselves in, we create stress because we are not experiencing what we would prefer to experience. Yet, at another level we are also attracted to our situation or circumstances. When we resist a situation we also accept it, for why would we reject it if we didn't also accept it. There would be no reason to reject it if we weren't also attracted to it. Rejection implies attraction. This simultaneous rejection and acceptance produces conflict and tension and this causes us stress.

Sometimes this is obvious. For example, when someone is giving up a habit such as smoking they struggle between wanting to give up yet not wanting to let go of their habit. Less obvious is the case of resisting a painful experience such as the loss of a loved one or feeling frustrated or bored in our work. But even in these cases, as much as we resist the new reality that confronts us, we are also compelled to accept it. We resist only what we also accept.

Attraction and resistance

Attraction is also an expression of an opposite feeling. If we observe the experience of attraction or desire we can also see how it expresses our resistance to having that to which we are attracted. The more we desire something, the greater the gulf between us and what we desire. Desire is a measure of the distance we must traverse in order to own, use or experience what we want.

Whenever we desire something, the desire keeps what we desire at some distance from us in just the same way that resistance keeps us away from things. The result of our desire is the same as when we reject something. We will get just so close, and how close we get is a measure of our resistance.

The belief: "I would like such-and-such" also contains a resistance to having what we would like. Ironically we can use attraction and desire to keep things at a distance. Letting go of attraction and desire also frees up our resistance so that we can simply enjoy and appreciate the experience to which we were initially attracted.

Self and other

If you have reflected on the nature of self-awareness, you have probably also discovered how an experience of our "self" co-exists with a belief that we are not our self. If you observe carefully, the moment you become aware of your "self" that self becomes an "other." Your "self" is not your self the moment you recognize it as your "self." When you know who you are, that which you know becomes an other. Ultimately, you are all that is not you. You are your self and an other at the same time. So, knowing your self means not knowing your self.

Similarly, as soon as you recognize your self as the subject who knows objects, you become an object for the subject that you do not know you are. At the very moment you experience yourself as the subject of your experience, the self becomes an object of your experience.

Some other examples of how beliefs co-exist (i.e. express and imply an opposite belief) are:

how we gain power through acknowledging our weaknesses;

how a belief that we are powerful creates a weakness;

how confusion is an expression of clarity (we know we are confused);

how a request for help demonstrates our resourcefulness and independence;

how defending something simultaneously invalidates it;

how saying: "This is safe," acknowledges a possible danger;

how saying: "This is dangerous," extends the boundaries of what we believe is an acceptable risk;

how we have a problem if we don't have any problems;

how it is not a problem to have a problem, since "life is just dealing with problems";

how acknowledging sadness can make us feel better. In saying: "I am sad" we could just as well be saying: "Now I feel good."

EXERCISE

Which of the above examples do you recognize? Can you think of other examples?

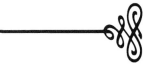

CHAPTER FIVE

Common conflicting beliefs

In a single day we experience a large number of conflicting beliefs. Even in the space of an hour we are immersed in a number of these beliefs. You could say we live in a soup of conflicting beliefs. Some of them describe our base-line condition of thinking. They operate in the background producing a low but nearly constant level of frustration or anxiety. Other conflicting beliefs produce more pronounced experiences of stress. Still others can produce critical and even life-threatening events in our lives.

EXERCISE

In this chapter we have listed a number of common conflicting beliefs and divided them into different categories. As you read the following lists of conflicting beliefs, tick the ones that occur in your own thinking. You may be surprised at how many of these conflicting beliefs you experience.

Concentrate on the beliefs that have occurred anytime in the last year. Also, it is not necessary to be aware of both the beliefs in a conflicting pair. For example, you may be aware that you often think: "Yes, I am fit and healthy." However, if this is a thought that crops up quite often in your thinking, then whether you realize it or not, you also have a concern that perhaps you are not fit and healthy. Similarly, if you find yourself thinking: "I can't trust so-and-so," then at some level you also believe that you can trust them.

So in completing this exercise, look for the types of thoughts that pop up in your thinking. If you are aware of only one pole of a pair of conflicting beliefs, then tick it, because the other pole will also be present.

Physical stresses

These are contradictory beliefs or attitudes about our body and physical condition. These beliefs produce an experience of physical stress and tension which can develop into physical pain and illness. Some examples are:

I'm healthy—I'm unhealthy.

I'm fat—I'm not fat.

I'm thin—I'm not thin.

I need a cigarette—I don't need a cigarette.

I need to get stoned—I don't need to get stoned.

I'm young—I'm old.

I need sex—I don't need sex.

I'm too young—I'm not too young.

I'm too old—I'm not too old.

I need a drink—I don't need a drink.

I am too tall—I'm not too tall.

I'm too short—I'm not too short.

I'm fit—I'm not fit.

I'm unfit—I'm not unfit.

I need to exercise—I don't need to exercise.

I'm sick—I'm not sick.

I'm tired—I'm not tired.

I'm comfortable—I'm uncomfortable.

I'm beautiful (or handsome)—I'm not beautiful.

I'm ugly—I'm not ugly.

This hurts—This doesn't hurt.

I'm sexy—I'm not sexy.

I'm exhausted—I'm not exhausted.

Intellectual stresses

Intellectual contradictions produce disturbing and burdensome thoughts. Some examples are:

I'm smart—I'm not smart.

I'm stupid—I'm not stupid.

I'm confused—I'm not confused,

I understand—I don't understand.

I'm wasting my time—I'm not wasting my time.

I'm learning—I'm not learning.

I'm special—I'm ordinary.

I'm prejudiced—I'm not prejudiced.

I'm careful—I'm careless.

I've achieved enough—I haven't achieved enough.

This is a waste of effort—This isn't a waste of effort.

I'm ambitious—I'm not ambitious.

I'm stubborn—I'm not stubborn.

I can wait—I can't wait.

It won't happen to me—It will happen to me.

I'm worthy—I'm unworthy.

I'm extravagant—I'm not extravagant.

I'm miserly—I'm not miserly.

I'm in control—I'm not in control.

I'm good—I'm bad.

I'm confident—I'm not confident.

I'm shy—I'm not shy.

I'm extroverted—I'm introverted.

This is fair—This is unfair.

This really matters—This doesn't really matter.

This will change—This won't change.

This will last—This won't last.

I created this—I didn't create this.

This is my fault—This isn't my fault.

I deserve this—I don't deserve this.

This is hard—This is easy.

I should do this—I shouldn't do this.

I don't need to do anything—I do need to do something.

I have enough—I don't have enough.

I will get this finished—I won't get this finished.

I made a mistake—I didn't make a mistake.

Emotional stresses

Emotional contradictions shape the negative moods and emotions we experience. They determine how we feel about ourselves and others. Some examples are:

I'm weak—I'm not weak.

I'm powerful—I'm not powerful.

I'm peaceful—I'm agitated.

I'm obsessed—I'm not obsessed.

I'm happy—I'm sad.

I need X—I don't need X.

I'm lovable—I'm unlovable.

Common conflicting beliefs

I'm disappointed—I'm not disappointed.

I can cope—I can't cope.

I'm resigned—I'm not resigned.

I love X—I don't love X.

I hate X—I don't hate X.

I like pressure—I don't like pressure.

I'm kind—I'm not kind.

I'm cruel—I'm not cruel.

I'm frightened—I'm not frightened.

I'm angry—I'm not angry.

I'm frustrated—I'm not frustrated.

I'm nervous—I'm not nervous.

I'm confident—I'm not confident.

I'm vulnerable—I'm not vulnerable.

I'm satisfied—I'm dissatisfied.

I'm sane—I'm insane.

This is boring—This is interesting.

This is painful—This is pleasurable.

This is dangerous—This is safe.

This is funny—This isn't funny.

This is serious—This isn't serious.

Social stresses

Social stresses are shaped by contradictions in our beliefs about our relationships with others. These contradictions produce interpersonal stresses and breakdowns in communication. They can be responsible for relationship problems, arguments, child abuse, environmental abuse, racial conflict, political conflict, murder and wars. Examples of social contradictions are:

I'm lonely—I'm not lonely.

I need more friends—I don't need more friends.

I'm independent—I'm dependent.

I love X—I hate X.

It matters—It doesn't matter.

I'm withholding—I'm not withholding.

I trust X—I don't trust X.

I'm jealous—I'm not jealous.

X is important—X isn't important.

I'm misunderstood—I'm not misunderstood.

I want children—I don't want children.

I'm weak—I'm not weak.

I'm powerful—I'm not powerful.

I'm too dominating—I'm not too dominating.

I'm too submissive—I'm not too submissive.

I'll be late—I won't be late.

X will be late—X won't be late.

I need to act—I don't need to act.

X is sensitive—X isn't sensitive.

I need a relationship—I don't need a relationship.

X can do it—X can't do it.

Someone else will do it—No one else will do it.

I must win—I mustn't win.

I must lose—I mustn't lose.

X will know—X won't know.

X hurt me—X didn't hurt me.

I forgive X—I don't forgive X.

X will help—X won't help.

I'm obliged to X—I'm not obliged to X.

I'm responsible—I'm irresponsible.

This is my responsibility—This is not my responsibility.

Spiritual stresses

Spiritual contradictions create religious and existential problems. Spiritual contradictions are also the source of the development of religious and spiritual traditions. However, these traditions are largely unsuccessful in resolving these contradictions since they inadvertently contribute to the conflicts they seek to resolve. Examples are:

I exist—I don't exist.

I am my body—I am not my body.

This is real—This is unreal.

This is rational—This is irrational.

I will survive my death—I won't survive my death.

I will be saved—I won't be saved.

There is hope—There is no hope.

There is a God—There isn't a God.

People are the same—People are different.

People are basically good—People are basically evil.

Existence is stressful—Existence isn't stressful.

This is perfect—This isn't perfect.

This is right—This is wrong.

This is how it should be—This isn't how it should be.

This is it—This isn't it.

Clarifying the conflicts

The above beliefs are examples of "contradicting beliefs." They are contradictory because they are opposites. There is another group of beliefs which are in conflict with each other but not actually contradicting each other. We call these "conflicting beliefs." "I have enough" and "I'm poor" are examples of conflicting beliefs.

Sometimes we are not aware of the contradicting beliefs that drive our stress. We may only be aware that we are in a soup of conflicting beliefs. The contradictions are disguised.

The most effective way to dissolve conflicting beliefs is to resolve them into a primary contradiction. Stress is most easily released when we discover the contradicting beliefs, since they induce the maximum stress. The diagrams below show how contradicting beliefs are diametrically opposed to each other while conflicting beliefs are tangentially opposed to each other. In the diagrams the arrows that are directly opposite each other represent contradicting beliefs. When the smaller arrow points towards the tip of a larger arrow, it shows examples of conflicting beliefs. Even so, all the beliefs, both the conflicting and contradicting ones, contribute to the experience of stress.

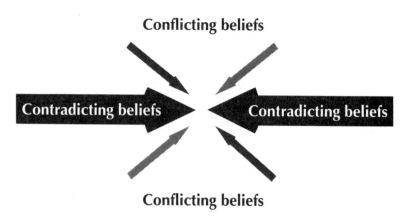

Conflicting beliefs

Contradicting beliefs   **Contradicting beliefs**

Conflicting beliefs

Conflicting and contradicting beliefs

In the second example, "I am healthy" and "I am unhealthy" are contradicting beliefs. In contrast, the beliefs "I feel young" and "I am unhealthy" are conflicting. They are in tension with each other even though they don't *directly* conflict. They are in tension because we usually associate "feeling young" with "being healthy."

The conflicting beliefs in the third example are: "This is easy" and "I can't finish this." "This is easy" and "I'm tired." "This is hard" and "I'm not tired." "This is hard" and "I can finish this."

Thinking and conflicting beliefs

The conflicting beliefs are by-products of the primary contradictions. Similarly, the primary contradictions also produce the incomplete, meandering and circuitous thoughts that run through our minds. These include memories of the past, assessments and interpretations of "what is happening now" and anticipations of the future.

Thoughts are like the surface traces of more fundamental conflicts. When we are in the middle of an intense conflict, our thinking can explode into a dense and chaotic stream of judgments and interpretations. As the conflicts become harmonized, the thoughts thin out and become more coherent. In a state of true harmony, our thinking is stable, light and controlled.

The daily grind

If you doubt that contradictory beliefs cause stress, consider how much time you spend in a day thinking about the types of dilemmas previously listed. Merely posing this question probably throws you into a dilemma: "Well, let me see. Yes, I do spend a lot of time in these sorts of conflicting beliefs. No, really it is just a little time. Actually, I'm not sure if I do or don't spend much time doing this. Yes, I'm pretty sure I don't spend a lot of time in these conflicting situations. But I'm doing it right now, so maybe I do spend a lot of time doing this. Maybe I spend all my time doing this. Perhaps it is the only thing I do. No, that's ridiculous. I spend very little time . . ." For most of us this sort of chatter goes on continuously, and we are mostly unaware of it and its wearing effect on us.

Each belief threatens the existence of the other. For example, if I believe I am intelligent, this belief is threatened by the belief that I am stupid. If I believe that the world is basically good, then this is threatened by the belief that the world is evil. Our beliefs conflict with each other, yet they also depend on each other. It is a little like the experience of the political prisoner who depends for his food and water on the same person who torments and tortures him.

The mind is a battleground

We experience these contradictions as a turbulent (and sometimes violent) battleground in which we attempt to maintain consistency in how we think about ourselves and the world. Our failure to think consistently is inevitable because thinking is inherently contradictory.

What happens is that two opposing beliefs act as though they are enemies to each other. Each belief takes territory in turn from the other and then (under threat) gives that same territory up. Each belief acts as though it can exist without the other. They behave as though they can exist by themselves. They act as though they have a right to exist quite independently of the other belief.

The battleground

The beliefs enter battle with each other. They tussle with each other, one having the upper edge for a time and then the other. Stress is caused by the simultaneous attraction and repulsion of conflicting beliefs. Our battles in and with the world are simply reflections of these internal battles.

These contradictory thoughts and judgments place us under constant stress as we try to gain and regain a stable and fixed set of beliefs about ourselves and the world. We become addicted to short-term relief by fixing onto one or other belief. We think: "Well, I will manage" and gain temporary relief from the stress of believing two contradictory things. Before long, however, we doubt our survival and so threaten a belief in our continuity.

Stress is so familiar, we are numb to it

This places us under tremendous pressure that is so constant and familiar that we no longer notice it. We only become aware of it when the stress erupts in a dramatic way or we can contrast our usual way of experiencing the world with the occasional moments of freedom we might experience when we are deeply relaxed and satisfied.

Periodically the turbulent background erupts in the form of emotional outbursts, anxiety, fear, moods of depression and resignation, physical illnesses, mental trauma, and in some instances, insanity.

We push threatening beliefs outside our awareness

We battle to keep opposing beliefs at a distance from each other. If necessary, we submerge one belief, pushing it outside our awareness by distracting ourselves. We cultivate strategies for remaining blind to the co-existence of conflicting beliefs.

But an opposite belief is always on our doorstep, pressing at the door of our awareness and challenging what we believe, while we try to keep it locked outside our minds.

QUERY

You say that I experience stress and conflict because I believe I must be good, loving, etc. and that I do this by suppressing the opposite beliefs. Are you suggesting that I should cultivate the opposite beliefs—that I am evil, unloving, etc?

ANSWER

No. Those negative beliefs are already there—they must be. What we suggest is that you stop denying you already have a belief that you are bad, unloving, and so forth. This is the first step to being able to resolve the conflict.

CHAPTER SIX

Harmonizing conflicting beliefs

The way to harmonize conflicting beliefs is simply to allow beliefs to return to their original and natural condition. When we release the effort that keeps our beliefs dis-connected, they spontaneously resolve into contradicting pairs and effortlessly dissolve into each other.

If thinking is left to itself, beliefs return to their source. If beliefs are left to themselves, unattached and unattended, they spontaneously resolve into contradicting pairs and then naturally and effortlessly dissolve into each other and return to their source. The *natural movement* is always towards the *dissolution of conflict*.

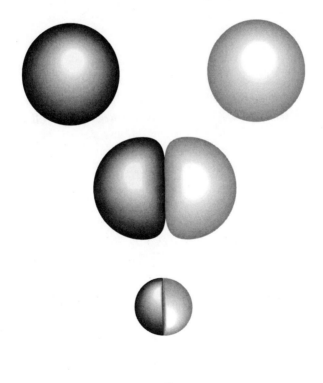

Harmonizing conflicting beliefs

Half the work has already been done

From one point of view we have already done half the work in harmonizing our beliefs since contradicting beliefs come together and collide in our thinking all the time. We saw this when we went through the lists of conflicting beliefs. These conflicting beliefs need not be a problem if we can allow them to blend and dissolve. Rather than trying to push our conflicting beliefs apart we can simply let them return to their natural, restful state. From this perspective, what we had previously opposed becomes an ally—a vital and most valuable tool. All we need to do is relax and let go of all effort to control and manipulate.

To say "it is a task" would be incorrect since there is no doing in this process. We cannot "let go" as something we do. We just allow what naturally occurs to occur without any interference or even real interest on our part.

CONCERN

If I use an opposite belief to dissolve a negative belief then the positive will evaporate along with the negative. What I want and need will dissolve along with what I don't want. If I use my positive beliefs to dissolve my negative beliefs, then I won't be left with any beliefs—bad or good!

ANSWER

"I won't be left with any beliefs" is a belief in itself. So are other fears such as: "I will lose everything" or "There won't be anything left." You can't have one belief without having the opposite. The belief that there won't be anything left if you get rid of all beliefs is only a problem because you believe that there will be nothing for you to experience—in which case there won't be nothing. There will be you with all your beliefs. In fact nothing will change—and this is what you also fear. If you fear that there will be nothing, you also fear that everything will be the same—as it always has been.

There are different levels at which we can resolve stressful beliefs. Ultimately we resolve our conflicting beliefs when we accept that beliefs can only exist with an opposite belief and allow a natural blending of opposites to occur.

There is a way of removing negative beliefs while keeping the positive. You can dis-connect the negative from the positive, but the process of maintaining the dis-connection is stressful.

If you still feel uncomfortable with the belief that "nothing will be left" were you to dissolve all your beliefs, then you can dissolve the belief that "nothing will be left" with the belief that "everything will be the same."

EXERCISE

Ponder the question: What will be left when you dissolve the belief that "Nothing will be left"?

QUESTION

Do we need our positive beliefs? Why do we need to believe that we are: brave, smart, kind, etc.?

ANSWER

We only need to be brave because we can be cowardly. If we couldn't be cowardly we wouldn't need to be brave. We would just be simple and natural. We need to believe we are smart because we fear believing that we are stupid. If we really knew we weren't stupid, we wouldn't have to tell ourselves that we are smart. We would simply do what we are capable of doing. We only need to believe we are kind in order to cover up our fear that we can be cruel. If we couldn't be cruel, there would be no need to be kind. We would just be appropriate.

CONSIDER

If you are neither cowardly nor heroic, how will you be?
If you are neither poor nor wealthy, how will you be?
If you think of yourself as neither stupid nor smart, how will you be?
Who would you rather deal with: someone who thinks of themselves as a hero, or someone who doesn't think in terms of being either a hero or a coward?
Who would you rather have as a friend: someone who needs to be kind or someone who is not hung up about being either cruel or kind?

Our positive beliefs only serve to consolidate negative beliefs. It is our refusal to give up positive beliefs that stops us removing negative beliefs. Once you release the negative beliefs, you no longer need the positive.

Hui Neng, a famous Chinese Zen master wrote that: "If there are no beliefs, there is not even an absence of beliefs."

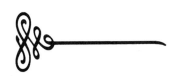

CHAPTER SEVEN

Phases of growth

This chapter describes a number of phases in the evolution of the state of Presence. Each phase corresponds to a different way that we hold our beliefs. They represent different degrees or levels of resolution of conflicting beliefs.

As our conflicting beliefs are harmonized, we move progressively through the phases. Chapter Four outlined how beliefs form, then separate and finally disconnect into two contradicting beliefs. The Phases of Growth track the inversion of this same process. Each phase corresponds to a movement in which conflicting beliefs return to an undifferentiated source.

The diagram on p. 90 traces this process through the different phases. Phase One, called *Dis-connection*, indicates a fundamental irresolution of conflicting beliefs and the final phase called *Presence* signifies the full harmonization of conflicting beliefs. This final phase is described separately in the next chapter.

Because our beliefs shape our experience, each phase also describes a different orientation and approach to living. Each phase has its own outlook, moods and possibilities.

The exercises incorporated in the practical course are specifically designed to facilitate movement through these different phases of growth.

There is no strict order in how we traverse these phases, though there is an overall sense of direction. They can represent a general pattern of growth over several years or even a lifetime. People are prone to jump from one phase to another in response to others, their own moods, opinions and different situations. In fact, all of them can be experienced in a day.

The illustrations at the beginning of each section depict the basic relationship of our beliefs for each phase.

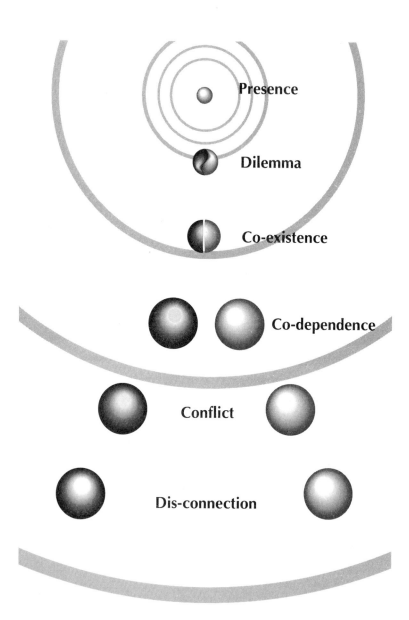

Presence

Dilemma

Co-existence

Co-dependence

Conflict

Dis-connection

The harmonization of beliefs and progress through the phases

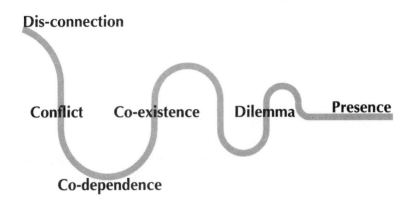

Phases of growth

PHASE 1 *Dis-connection*

The first phase, which we call Dis-connection, rests on a powerful belief in a fundamental separation between us and the world. Once we believe that we are separate from the world, we can become dis-connected from it and also dis-connected from ourselves.

Dis-connection is based on fear

Dis-connection is driven by fear—either fear of ourselves or fear of the world. When we fear ourselves, we are thrown into the world in order to lose ourselves. When we fear the world, we retreat into ourselves in order to avoid the world. We tend to become totally preoccupied—either with ourselves or with the world.

The bottom line in both styles of dis-connection is to avoid anything sharp, painful, or even remotely uncomfortable, touching us—be that negative thoughts or other people.

Dis-connection from the world

When we are dis-connected from the world, other people show up as threats to our autonomy and integrity. We will hide out from other people—sometimes quite literally. We may go to great lengths to avoid specific people or situations.

We view the world as hostile and threatening

We live our lives as though we are open to constant contamination, as if we are in a hostile environment that continually threatens us. Always looking over our shoulder, always on the look-out, we sense that some threat is just around the corner. Consequently, we are grossly constricted in the relationships we are able to form.

The people we do attract aren't attracted for their own worth and humanness, but rather for their role in confirming and validating our own limited identity. Really we aren't interested in other people, though from time to time we need to announce to people who we are and what we stand for.

There is a mood of paranoia, desperation, isolation and claustrophobia about the Phase of Dis-connection, since we are driven by the fear that if we don't continually protect ourselves we will disappear.

We might surround ourselves with our own familiar

thoughts—the memorabilia of our dank, dark and oh-so-familiar world. Or we might become immersed in self-improvement programs, commit ourselves to long-term therapy or struggle to achieve spiritual purity.

We become preoccupied with ourselves

In the Phase of Dis-connection, we become so preoccupied with ourselves, so immersed in the exploration and experience of who we are, that we are effectively paralyzed—and no longer able to act powerfully and competently.

We struggle to either stay the same or to totally transform ourselves. Either way there is no acceptance of who we are and how we are changing (or not changing).

We try to protect our beliefs

To keep our beliefs safe and secure we will go to any lengths. We refuse to test them in the world and actively insulate them from alternative viewpoints. If, for example, we believe that we are honest and trustworthy, we refuse to listen to any suggestion that we could be untrustworthy. We refuse to hear an alternative point of view. We simply won't have anything to do with people who threaten our autonomy—for us they don't exist.

In this phase we seek pure experiences—pure pleasure, absolute perfection, pure power, complete independence, absolute moral goodness, total health, etc.—all uncontaminated by the slightest trace of their opposite.

We figure that in order to be good, we mustn't be bad—not even slightly. We look for the smallest injustice in order to invalidate other people or we hold onto a single evil thought in order to destroy our own self-worth. We will destroy our own pleasures because they have been contaminated or interrupted by some small external interference.

Dis-connection from ourselves

The other type of dis-connection is dis-connection from ourselves. We do this by getting caught up in the world. The fear of being with ourselves drives us to lose ourselves by becoming immersed in the world.

We lose ourselves in our work

We lose ourselves in our work, having to be always in action. Our behavior becomes erratic, incoherent and inconsistent when we lose contact with who we are. Perhaps we jump from project to project, keeping busy in order to stay dis-connected from who we are. It's as if we throw ourselves totally into the world.

At work we may know only how to bust our guts or collapse in a heap on the floor through exhaustion. There is no time to be with ourselves. The only choices are to be totally distracted or unconscious. There is no sense of balance or grace in how we manage our affairs.

We pursue impossible dreams

This type of dis-connection is also characterized by narrow-minded pursuits. However, here we only seek external achievements. For example, we may vow to become a millionaire before year's end, or indulge ourselves totally in physical pleasures. Or we might simply try to be the perfect parent—every single moment of the day. It doesn't particularly matter whether we are being pure or indulgent, we are trapped and blinded by our single-minded pursuit of an external, impossible goal.

Internal dis-connection

This phase is also marked by an internal dis-connection—a dismemberment of our personality. Our feelings are dis-connected from our thinking. Our behavior is dis-connected from who we really are. We may be unable to say what we feel at any moment. Our feelings become just one big blur. We are either totally in-our-heads and dis-connected from our feelings, or so immersed in, and overpowered by, our feelings, that sometimes we cannot even talk.

Time feels solid

In this phase time feels solid. A day is lived as a "block of time." We may wake up in a particular mood and carry it with us throughout the day until we go to sleep at night.

If we have time to "fill in" it is a "disaster." We don't know what to do. If we find ourselves stretched for time, it is a "catastrophe." We don't know how to reschedule an appointment. It doesn't even occur to us as a possibility that we could rearrange our commitments.

We are dis-connected from time. It is something "out there" and it runs its own course independently of us.

PHASE 2 Conflict

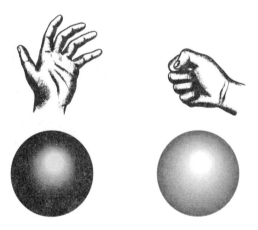

At some point during the Phase of Dis-connection we begin to acknowledge and feel the fear that drives this experience. We allow ourselves to be vulnerable. If we have contracted into our inner world, we will begin to look outside. We transcend the fear of being with others and renounce our privacy. If we have become lost in the worlds of other people, we take stock and begin to gain a sense of who we are.

These movements signal a new pull towards expansion—an evolutionary growth, either in terms of new relationships or a deeper understanding of ourselves.

Although this phase is evolutionary, it is a highly conflictual state because we are still living out of our old style of contraction. The two forces of expansion and contraction produce stress and conflict. We begin to expand our horizons, but we still feel a need to protect ourselves. Part of us would dearly love to stay in our shell, in our comfortable cocoon, but we feel an urge to grow. We can no longer ignore that there are points of view different from our own. It is clear that wherever we go, the shadow of conflicting opinions follows.

This phase has a rough and aggressive quality about it as we brush up against circumstances and people who are seen as a hindrance and threat to our security and way of life. Our hope for complete autonomy or oblivion-in-the-world are now constantly challenged and as the challenges intensify, we find ourselves forced to respond. Ordinarily we would have some choice. We could take flight and retreat (dis-connect), move forward by modifying our objectives and forming alliances (co-dependence) or stand our ground and fight.

We fight for what we believe in

However, in the midst of this phase we have no choice but to fight for our beliefs. The only way we know how to deal with something different is to locate an opponent and fight it. At this point we have no choice but to attempt to destroy it while surviving ourselves.

We find fault in others

Consequently, we may find constant fault in others. We make them wrong in order for us to be right, or we make others right in order to invalidate ourselves. At the very least, we struggle to avoid associating with people who stimulate conflicting thoughts or feelings in us.

We may constantly judge ourselves

The other option is to fight the battle internally, within our own world of thoughts and feelings. In this case we torment ourselves by continually dissecting our thoughts, feelings and behavior—judging whether they are good or bad, right or wrong.

The habits of our style of dis-connection also follow us into this phase. If we are prone to dis-connect from ourselves, then conflict may take the form of sacrificing ourselves by fighting for some cause—be this a team, a company, a religion or a nation. If we are predisposed to dis-connect from the world, the point comes where we can no longer ignore the world. We are impelled to fight for the survival of our opinions, values and finally for our selves. For example, we may forsake our marriage in order to pursue a private career or give up our job in order to retire to the country.

Being and doing

This phase is also marked by a conflict between the internal and external styles of living. The conflict is between being and doing. When we are in action in the world, we wish we could retreat inside. Then when we are with ourselves all we can do is think about what we should do next.

If we are by nature introspective and self-satisfied, the fear is still there that we will lose our footing if we throw ourselves into relationships and projects. So we make forays into the world, but rush back to the still point within for nourishment. We can't see how we could be nourished by our work.

Conversely, if by nature we are extroverted, then in this phase we begin to seek refuge from the complex and consuming relationships or the overly ambitious projects that punctuate our life. However, try as we might to nourish ourselves through therapy, meditation or just making time for ourselves we are magnetically drawn back into external concerns.

We are thrown from one extreme to the other. The only choice is to try to be composed and quiet, savoring the essence of our being, or to become caught up in the lives and work of others. There is no middle ground.

In this phase it doesn't matter what we do. We are continually plagued by the thought: "This isn't what I'm meant to be doing."

Time is an enemy

In this phase, time is perceived as an enemy. Time is an obstacle, a barrier that constrains us and which we have to break through. We will find ourselves under- or over-scheduling commitments, caught between having too much or too little time.

Similarly, space is experienced as a commodity. Either we want more space or less space. Space either constrains us—we feel hemmed in—or it is a barrier to be overcome. People are either too close or too distant.

PHASE 3 Co-dependence

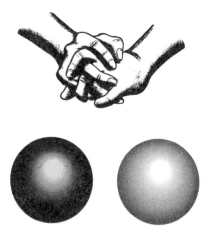

Transition into this phase occurs as a response to the aggression and exhaustion that characterizes the Conflict Phase. Rather than fight a fabricated enemy, we now change tack and decide to adjust our identity in ways that will allow us to live in a world of different values, beliefs and opinions. We give up fighting and fall into Co-dependence.

In this way, Co-dependence is also a reaction to dis-connection. From the Conflict Phase we could retreat into isolation (dis-connection), but the memories of that phase still persist, so we shift our stance and begin to resolve our conflicts by adjusting to accommodate the conflicts.

However, the difference between Dis-connection and Co-dependence is significant. If, for example, in the Dis-connection Phase we seek refuge by retreating from the world, then, in the Co-dependent Phase our isolation and loneliness depend upon having people around to actively ignore us.

We need others for our pleasure and pain

Though this phase begins with the simple adjustment of our beliefs in order to accommodate conflict and difference, before long our beliefs become entwined in a constricting and limiting way. We begin to depend on others for our pleasure and pain. Our well-being and sense of self cannot occur independently of others. We learn to dance so well with our partners that we get trapped and blinded by our own skill. Ultimately the survival of our identity depends on our interactions with other people.

We experience the "disease of lost selfhood." In the midst of this phase we focus exclusively outside ourselves for our experience of self-worth (be that positive or negative), and for our values, beliefs and needs.

We seek external approval

We might constantly seek approval from others. Or we may use others to inflict the pain and suffering which we "deserve" through our own beliefs about our guilt and lack of self-worth. Whatever it is that we need, we get others to do it to us—be this to hate us, love us, dominate us or ignore us.

Perhaps we surround ourselves with people who are weak

and pathetic in order to confirm our own power and domination. Or we may be thrown into relationships with people who are cruel and insensitive in order to confirm our kindness and sensitivity.

There is no room for individual change

In this phase we may be trapped in a job or unable to extricate ourselves from dysfunctional relationships because they precisely and accurately serve the needs upon which we are dependent. Our relationships seem to fit like a glove to the point that there is no room for individual change or growth. If we grow, it is cause for a breakdown, a catastrophe, for those around us. If they grow, it is a problem for us.

Internal co-dependence

This Co-dependence Phase also manifests internally as an inability to separate our thinking and feelings. It may be that we can't think or speak clearly in the face of powerful emotions. Our thinking is so dependent on our moods and feelings that if we are feeling excited our thinking is necessarily scattered and all over the place. If we are feeling threatened, we have no choice but to be tongue-tied. We cannot dis-connect our thinking from our feelings.

From the other angle, if we are in a racy conversation we have no choice but to get swept up in the mood of excitement. We cannot both participate in the conversation and keep centered.

Our moods and emotions can't function independently of each other. We may have to induce a mood of panic before we can move into action. Or we may need to get angry before we can be intimate with someone. The expression of each mood depends on expressing other moods.

Time controls us

In this Phase we also become dependent on time and space. We can become tied to time in a way that leaves little room for impulse and spontaneity. Time controls us and distance is always a limiting factor. Perhaps everything has to be organized weeks, even months, in advance. Our movements always need to be the most economical. We might begin to behave like the famous 18th-century German philosopher Immanuel Kant who never ventured more than a couple of miles from the place of his birth and who followed a life of such extreme regularity that the people of his village would set their clocks by his daily consti-tutional walk. Though he lived alone he was wedded to time and tied to his physical surroundings.

PHASE 4 Co-existence

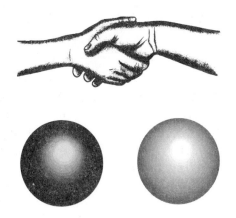

At some point during the Co-dependent Phase, we see the compromising nature of this co-dependence. We recognize the distortion of our personality which has been caused by accom-modating the needs and concerns of other people. Also we see the possibility of living in respectful and mutually empowering relationships. This signals entry into the Co-existence Phase.

Co-existence is a wonderful phase of personal development, for it bridges all levels of coping. It begins at the point where we can adequately cope with ourselves, our work and our relationships, and reaches right through to very elegant, empowering and socially rewarding ways of participating in and contributing to life.

Fine-tuning our judgments

Progress through this phase is measured by an increasing acceptance of the circumstances in which we find ourselves and a growing capacity to fine-tune the judgments we make about ourselves and the world.

In this phase we no longer make global judgments. No longer are we driven to think about ourselves or respond to others in simplistic, black and white categories. People, groups, professions, races are no longer regarded as merely good or bad. Our judgments gain more and more texture. We distinguish and discriminate how and when we are being responsible or irresponsible, caring or indifferent, competent or incompetent.

Keeping an eye on the ball

However, throughout this phase there is still a sense of needing to manage the whole affair. At the beginning there is a strong sense of having to work at it in order to manage our work and relationships, but even when we reach the level of being a master there is a sense of effort and application. We may design and orchestrate our lives in a masterful and elegant way, but we still have to constantly work at it—making evaluations, formulating plans, designing actions, correcting and adjusting, dealing with breakdowns, and so on. Others may see our work and relationships as smooth, easy and rewarding, but from the inside we are still planning, calculating, anticipating and living in terms of a game-plan or strategy. We still feel a need to keep an eye on the ball.

Our competence is tied to the acquisition of relevant skills— skills in managing our moods, our relationships, our career, negotiating mutually satisfactory outcomes, etc. We can even learn to design our moods to assist our thinking and use thoughts to modify our feelings and emotions, but still our competence and ease of living are a function of learning. To do better we need to know more, and then have more practice.

Nevertheless, this phase can bring us to the very brink of living a satisfied and rewarding life.

PHASE 5 Dilemma

This next phase may begin gently as a feeling of perplexity, mild confusion or uncertainty; or it may begin dramatically as the culmination of an emotional or intellectual crisis. It can occur in the midst of a mid-life crisis or as little more than an intellectual quandary.

Similarly, this phase can be experienced as a drawn out emotional struggle for meaning and solidity or as the final residue of an intellectual search for clarity and certainty.

On the path of self-development, a point is reached where we begin to lose our sense of progress and direction. It could be that things are being managed so easily and automatically that we begin to wonder who is doing this, or whether we need to be doing anything at all. We are not sure whether we are at work or on a permanent holiday.

Questioning who we really are

This phase could also start with the realization that we are somewhere totally different from where we thought we were. We might wake up one day and find ourselves in a thoroughly boring job or relationship that just yesterday had captured all our passion and energy. We begin to question who we are and what we are doing at a very fundamental level.

The very notion of making progress seems elusive. What would constitute progress and where are we going anyway? We may question: "Am I going forwards, backwards or standing still?" and have no real way of telling which direction we are going. We may well want to retreat or go forwards, but we also sense that such moments could take us anywhere—or nowhere. We find ourselves wanting to hold on and let go at the same time.

In this phase our feelings can become so bare and open that we can't tell what we are feeling. It could be love or it could be hatred. Our sensitivity is so acute that at the very same time and place we feel love there is hatred. It is as though our sensitivity and openness include yet transcend love and hatred.

This sensitivity extends to the environment. Perhaps we begin to notice that every time we register pleasure there is a sense of hurt or damage and pain. This is particularly apparent if we are attached to the pleasure. The fear of a pleasurable experience ending can produce pain. At the same time, pain can have a desirable, even enjoyable, quality to it.

What is real or illusion?

This phase can be accompanied by a whole range of moods and emotions. It can be perplexing and disconcerting because we don't know what it is we are getting or what it is we are losing. Are they the same thing or different?

The more we find ourselves being infused with a new energy and insight, the more we are at a loss to say what it is we are really gaining. Our awareness seems to expand to the point where it completely disappears. Perhaps what we are gaining is nothing! The experience is both deeply profound yet totally meaningless. We are not sure whether this is the most real thing we have ever experienced or if it is a total illusion. The *Lankavatara Sutra* expresses this dilemma by saying:

"Reality is not as it seems and nor is it otherwise."

As our sense of awareness increases, we also find ourselves losing every thought and conception we ever had about the goals we have been seeking. This experience can be simultaneously exhilarating and unnerving, for as we continue to lose hope of ever finding our most cherished goals, we seem to be gaining everything we could ever want.

We also notice that if we try to make "letting go" of our hope and ambitions a technique to produce or maintain this experience, we begin to lose what we already have. We might find ourselves in the double-bind of wanting to let go of all our desires and of trying to let go of any effort.

We are not sure whether it is something we *are* doing or are *not* doing that is bringing it on. All our efforts to figure it out, to understand what is happening, are fruitless. On the one hand our experience seems to be related to what we are thinking, but we also sense that it has nothing to do with what we are thinking or feeling. It is not clear whether we are causing it—or whether someone or something else is responsible. It can be terrifying that there is nothing we can do to bring it on or destroy it.

We get the feeling that we are not going to be around to have this ultimate experience. We also sense that we won't get it while we are hanging around. This could be the biggest disappointment of our entire life. Just when we are on the verge of getting it—that final insight, that ultimate goal—we go out to lunch!! Is this the cosmic joke?

Finally, we realize that there is nowhere to go, nowhere to retreat to or move forward into. There is nowhere to be, other than where we are. There is no one to be except the person we are. We come home to who we are and where we have always been. This moment—which requires no effort, change, or movement—signals the transition to the final phase. It is letting go and accepting what has always been.

This transition may or may not occur. And there is no way of telling whether or not it will happen since there is nothing we can do to make it happen, or to stop it from happening. Doing anything to make it happen—including doing nothing—is quite immaterial to the emergence of the final phase.

EXERCISE

Locate the five most important relationships in your life at this time. On separate sheets, write the name of each person. Spend five or so minutes writing about your relationship with each person. Write "automatically"—don't stop to think first, simply note down your immediate thoughts, ideas, and feelings. When you've run out of automatic thoughts, stop.

Now reflect on the five phases of growth outlined in this chapter. With these in mind, assess which of the different phases each relationship is in. The relationship may bridge phases or may oscillate between different phases. Some dimensions of the relationship may be in one phase while other dimensions may be in others. You may learn things about these relationships that you hadn't recognized before.

On the following pages is a chart which describes some of the typical conversations that occur in each phase. This will help you to locate the phases that typify your various relationships.

If you wish to go further with this exercise, you may like to investigate which specific conflicting beliefs dominate or at least recur within your important relationships.

Typical conversations in each phase of growth

EMOTIONS	GENERIC CONVERSATIONS

Dis-connection

Isolation	What's the point in this?
Rejection	I give up.
Fear	This is ridiculous.
Distraction	I'm nervous.
Separation	This is dangerous.
	S/he has no idea who I am.
	S/he has no idea how I'm feeling.
	I don't care about . . .
	I don't give a stuff about how s/he is seeing me.
	It is no business of theirs how I'm feeling.

Conflict

Anger	I'm pissed off.
Vindictiveness	It's their fault.
Blame	I'll get back at them.
	S/he is trying to make it difficult for me.

Co-dependence

Dependence	I have to please X.
Neediness	I can't do this without X.
Boredom	What will X think if I . . .
	I'll ask X if I can do this.

Co-existence

Vigilance	I'm getting better at this.
Application	I can see what I need to change.
Ambition	That didn't work so I'll change it.
Learning	I'm feeling better.
	I'm making progress.
	I'm getting closer.
	I'm learning how to do this.
	What else can I change?

Dilemma

Confused	I don't know if I'm making any progress
Perplexed	with this or not.
Spaced-out	Should I keep doing this the same or do
Anxious	something different?
	This is absurd.
	There is nothing to do!
	What am I supposed to do?
	I'm totally lost.
	This is it—isn't it?
	Should I continue or stop?

Presence

Aware
Alert
Relaxed
Calm
Present

CHAPTER EIGHT

Presence

It is difficult to be specific about the final phase called Presence because language can't adequately describe it. Intriguingly, throughout the ages, thousands of people have spent millions of words trying to describe the state of Presence. Some have used words in an effort to say *nothing* about this state of existence. Others have remained silent as a way of trying to say *something* about it. However, what they have said or not said neither adds to nor subtracts from our understanding of this state. None of the descriptions are more or less accurate.

So if you are hoping to understand this phase by reading this chapter, then give up. Stop reading! *Trying* to understand will only stop you from experiencing it. If you read this with even the slightest hope that it may help you understand Presence, then your reading is totally pointless. It can't help you achieve what you say you are seeking.

Alternatively, if you try to understand this phase by "stopping reading", by just deciding to let the experience emerge, organically, of its own accord, this is equally hopeless. This is no different from reading, since you are still trying to do something to get it. So, stop reading, or if you prefer, continue. It makes no difference what you decide. You cannot understand it, and you cannot get it by trying to understand it.

It isn't personal

Presence isn't a personal phenomenon. It is misleading to talk about someone having it in the same way we might say that someone is perceptive or very learned. Presence can't be owned or possessed. It isn't merely the capacity to get one's way or influence people. Those who have it don't know it as a possession, a quality or an achievement since there is no one there to own it. Only those who haven't got it—who view it in others or see it as a future achievement for themselves—make it personal, and what they make personal isn't Presence.

We cannot find Presence

The state of Presence cannot be found by looking for it. Why? Because it isn't anywhere for us to look to find it. It cannot be found outside of us. Nor can it be found inside us. It isn't located in the deepest recesses of our mind. It isn't in the heavens or somehow pervading the world we experience. Nor is it *not* in these places. It is here in this very space where we are right now.

We cannot gain it

Since Presence isn't created or produced, we can't gain it. We can't obtain it by seeking to get what someone else has got. We can't get it by looking for what we haven't got. The *Tao Te Ching* says:

> It cannot be gained through attachment.
> It cannot be gained through detachment.
> It cannot be gained through advantage.
> It cannot be gained through disadvantage.
> It cannot be gained through esteem.
> It cannot be gained through humility.

There is nothing we can do—or not do—in order to be Present. Presence represents the moment-by-moment acceptance and letting go of whatever we are experiencing, not as a strategy, but as a spontaneous and effortless response to life. Some may see this state manifest in all sorts of miraculous ways. We might see people in this state as always being in the right place, at the right time, meeting all the right sorts of people. If this is how we see the state of Presence, it is because in this state there is no right place, right time or right group of people. Others will see Presence as a supremely ordinary and natural way of being.

There is no thought, or mood, or attitude, or outlook that signifies that we are Present or not Present. So thinking: "Ah! Now I'm Present" hasn't anything to do with being Present. When we think such a thought we might be Present and we might not.

Presence entails being available to experience any thought, mood, attitude or outlook that happens to be there. Whether the thoughts and feelings are good or bad, blissful or miserable, peaceful or agitated, exciting or boring, we let them be exactly as they are. We don't approve of some and reject others. We don't praise or blame ourselves for however we are being. Our thoughts and feelings are neither good nor bad. They are simply the thoughts and feelings that they are.

The point is not to suppress our experience nor charge it up, but just to let it be, simply and fully appreciating our thoughts, feelings and sensations as they are without any need for meddling or interference. This outlook is always fresh and open and above all suspicion and mistrust since there is nothing to defend or attack. At this level, our experience becomes seamless since the capacity to let go—moment-by-moment—with complete detachment, smooths out any jarring or even unsettling experiences.

Some people try to experience Presence by going beyond their thoughts or beliefs and connecting with their bare experience, but this has nothing to do with Presence. Why? Because to do this is an intentional and excluding action. In transcending thought one is trying to avoid one thing (thinking) and recover something else (our experience). Presence has nothing to do with going beyond or transcending thoughts and beliefs. It is being Present to whatever is manifesting.

If we understand Presence as an injunction or direction to do anything or be in a particular way, this is *not* Presence since there is no purpose, meaning or even value in being Present. Presence is "simply being."

This is a new way of living in which we are totally fulfilled, moment by moment, and genuinely free of burdensome thoughts and conflicting emotions. This is the freedom that cuts through the illusions of believing we can be somewhere different from where we are, or someone other than who we are.

When we are authentically present to our thoughts, feelings and perceptions, we are intrinsically free. We experience a freedom that allows us to be fully where we are rather than needing to escape or deny any aspect of ourselves or what we are experiencing. This experience doesn't have degrees. It is inconceivable that it could be better. This simply isn't a consideration because it stands entirely outside the domain of assessments and comparisons. It is an experience so totally removed from our usual considerations of correcting, enhancing or improving what we are experiencing as to make it simultaneously spiritual yet undeniably real.

Nor can we lose it

Finally, Presence cannot be lost since it can be neither created nor destroyed. If we think we've lost our sense of Presence, then whatever it is that we think we've lost, it is not our Presence. It must be something else—most probably a particular feeling of clarity or calm.

Thinking that we've lost our Presence is simply "thinking" that we've lost our Presence. It is a little like thinking: "It would be nice to go home now" midway through a day at the office.

Even if you define Presence by the characteristic that you can't get it or lose it, you still can't lose it because it cannot be defined.

CHAPTER NINE

Natural Release

Natural Release is the phenomenon of beliefs automatically and spontaneously resolving into pairs of opposites and dissolving into nothing. However, this is a limited and deceptive description, for it sounds as though this is an *event* that occurs in time. This description is trying to explain something that occurs constantly and moment-by-moment. Another way to explain it is to say that in Natural Release *nothing* happens, because when it occurs we are not attempting to explain or understand how or why we are being "simply Present." This is Natural Release as Presence.

Trying to explain or interpret Natural Release at this level is paradoxical. For example, in the practical course we have developed, some participants break through to an experience of Presence in which Natural Release happens automatically and transparently. In trying to describe it, they sometimes say that the experience doesn't have anything to do with the course or exercises they have been doing. It is as though the very exercises that they may have been doing minutes before are unrelated to what they are presently experiencing. The exercises can seem pointless—even ridiculous—after one has achieved this breakthrough.

But, paradoxically, the possibility of this breakthrough occurring is greatly enhanced by fully participating in the course. For some people, it is only through participating in the course that they gain such an experience. So while it is true that the breakthrough experience is unrelated to the exercises it is also true that the exercises prepare the participants for the breakthrough experience.

The Natural Release method

The main exercise that prepares participants for an experience of Presence is a method that is also called Natural Release. This method is called Natural Release because it consciously simulates the process of de-energizing dis-connected beliefs, thereby allowing conflicting beliefs to return to their original undifferentiated condition. It is a very gentle method for releasing stress and conflict because, in essence, all it requires is releasing the energy that fractures our thinking and causes us to believe conflicting things.

The Natural Release method can be taught and learned. It involves blending the energy of conflicting beliefs. This allows the beliefs to fold in on each other, as it were. When they dissolve into each other, we experience a natural release of any residual stress and tension.

When the method is used elegantly and skillfully, it produces a sublime experience of alert and relaxed Presence. The actual deployment of the method is exquisite in its own right. Because the method mirrors the most natural and direct pathway for harmonizing conflict, it quickly begins to happen automatically. People who use the method report that they are able to just sit back and watch—in wonder and joy—as limiting beliefs and potentially constricting emotions automatically invoke an opposite belief or emotion. Then these coalesce and evaporate into nothing. They arrive at a point where stress and conflict are automatically released the very instant they might otherwise have formed, without needing to rely on any technique or guideline.

At this point they are not using Natural Release as a method. Instead they are simply observing and appreciating what we all do when we authentically resolve conflict as opposed to temporarily holding it at bay by suppressing a belief that conflicts with our preferred way of seeing things. While this stage of appreciating Natural Release is delightful, people soon go beyond it. From here on they simply experience a deep sense of inner harmony as Natural Release occurs transparently and automatically.

If a need to use the method arises when one is in this state, one can gently invoke the methods of Natural Release to dissolve the limitation that one *needs* to use this method. In fact, it is a good idea for people to release the need to use Natural Release as soon as they recognize that it is a method that they are becoming dependent on.

In the practical course we also recommend that participants release any limiting beliefs that they might have acquired in earlier phases of their work. For example, participants might have acquired a belief that stress is caused by conflicting beliefs, since we talk about stress in this way in this book. To the extent that someone continues to believe that stress is indeed caused by conflicting beliefs, we invite them to release this belief by seeing that this belief implies the opposite belief, that stress has nothing to do with conflicting beliefs. Participants then release the belief that stress is caused by conflicting beliefs. When this belief is released, conflicting beliefs can be present without causing stress. Conflicting beliefs are simply conflicting beliefs. In fact, it is also only a belief that any two beliefs conflict with each other.

Releasing mind

The Natural Release method is based on being able to access a level of consciousness we've called the Releasing Mind. Participants in the practical course learn to experience the Releasing Mind through a series of simple exercises that are briefly described in Appendix Two. The Releasing Mind is a foundational level of consciousness. It is the level of consciousness where stress and conflict first emerge and it is the level of consciousness that is the lubricant, as it were, for the dissolution of stress and conflict. It is a subtle consciousness in that while it can be experienced, it doesn't have any obvious content. It can be likened to air. Air is the most basic, immediate and essential source for our nutrition and existence, yet we can easily forget its existence and ignore its importance.

Beyond method

As people gain competence in Natural Release, they quickly learn not to over-use the method. Firstly, they *practice* Natural Release in order to enter a more spacious and peaceful way of being, but once they are in this state they do not tamper or interfere with it by unnecessarily using the procedures that got them there. They appreciate how the automatic and natural release of conflict can be interrupted by using the Natural Release method; and they enjoy the ease and simplicity of their natural condition. In fact, when people are in a real state of Presence, it is impossible to *practice* Natural Release because it is completely irrelevant.

However, when the experience of Natural Release begins to dissipate, they gently invoke the method again, but only to the point where Natural Release is functioning automatically.

Another valuable skill that is quickly acquired by formally practicing Natural Release is the ability to recognize it as an experience that is always available to us. Each time we energize a conflictual situation we also have an opportunity to let it return to a harmonious state. For example, prior to stepping into an argument, there is always a point where we are also able to let things be.

In time we grow to appreciate the natural ease and universal presence of this process. We begin to feel the seed of harmony that lies at the heart of every conflict and we learn to support the natural harmonization of conflict by lightly anticipating the interdependence, blending and dissolving of conflicting beliefs before they push us around and throw us into alienating and painful situations.

APPENDIX ONE

Origins

This appendix is primarily for readers who have an interest in the historical origins of the ideas and methods in this book.

The framework presented in this book is a contemporary and modern synthesis of ideas and methods that have originated in India, China and Tibet over the last 2500 years. For the most part we have drawn on Buddhist traditions, though many of the ideas can also be found in Taoist philosophy. We view the book as one more step in a lineage of practical wisdom that has been cultivated, refined and transmitted in India and Asia for well over 3000 years.

After writing this book, we recognized that its structure essentially follows a time-honoured method for describing the human condition that was first formulated by the Buddha. This method is called the four facts or principles of spiritual elevation (*arya-satya*). It is a sequence of explanation that is used in all traditions of Buddhism to describe the human predicament and suggest solutions to our problems. In traditional accounts the four facts are:

1. There is suffering.

2. Suffering has a cause.

3. Because it has a cause, a cessation of suffering is possible.

4. There is a method for stopping suffering. The method is described in many different ways in Buddhism, but ultimately it involves cultivating the middle path that avoids the extremes of accepting or rejecting what we experience.

Our modern interpretation of the spiritual endeavor can be viewed as a reformulation of these four facts. This reformulation allows us to integrate the most powerful and effective methods that have been developed in Buddhism into one simple and coherent system. In our interpretation they are:

1. Living can be stressful.

2. Stress is caused by conflicting beliefs.

3. Conflicting beliefs can be harmonized—resulting in presence.

4. The method is natural release.

This reformulation incorporates and integrates the most important features of Basic Buddhism (the Nikaya tradition), the Middle Path (Madhyamika) and the Complete Fulfillment (rDzogs chen). Thus, in this book and the course that accompanies it, we have brought theoretical and practical continuity to three of the most significant and quintessential traditions in Buddhism.

By discovering the interface and compatibility between these three traditions, we have been able to develop a system of personal and social development that is enhanced by combining three already highly effective methodologies.

In particular, we have been able to join the structural power of the Middle Path (Madhyamika) with the ease, acceptance and organic flavor of the Complete Fulfillment perspective. In this process of adaptation, we have emphasised the affective as opposed to the logical aspects of the Middle Path. In the traditional Middle Path, the reciprocal deconstruction of opposite beliefs is driven by an analytical logic that is used in both dialectical and contemplative settings. The practical program we have developed is based on the recognition and balancing of "emotional paradoxes".

For those who are interested to further note the connections between the Buddhist traditions and our interpretation, we will point out some of the more important correspondences.

1. Stress and tension are the equivalent of *duhkha*, which has traditionally been translated as suffering or unsatisfactoriness.

2. The term presence is our translation of *vidya* (Tib. *rig pa*). This is a term used in the Complete Fulfillment (rDzogs chen) tradition to refer to a state of pure and unsullied awareness in which we are present to whatever is.

3. The critical concept and role of "beliefs" corresponds to a number of related Buddhist terms such as *drshti*—viewpoint or opinion, *paksha*—position, *pratijna*—thesis.

4. The idea that beliefs shape our experience of the world is contained in the Middle Path notion that the world exists through the force of linguistic designation *(prajnapti-sat)*.

5. The observation that stress is caused by conflicting beliefs is a neglected aspect of the Middle Path philosophy that was first developed in the second century in India by Nagarjuna. In general, Buddhist scholars have not yet seen how this idea makes complete sense of the Middle Path paradoxes *(prasanga)* that deconstruct logically opposed positions. A full explanation of this methodology can be found in Peter Fenner, *The Ontology of the Middle Way*, Dordrecht, Holland: Kluwer Publications, 1990. A comprehensive model of the cognitive changes that occur when using the Middle Path method in a traditional setting can be found in Peter Fenner, *Reasoning into Reality*, Boston, Mass.: Wisdom Publications, 1994.

6. The observation that beliefs form in pairs of logical opposites is found in Buddhism and Taoism. This idea is formally captured in the *apoha* theory of meaning developed by Buddhist philosophers in the fifth century which states that things are defined by what they are not. The actual process whereby beliefs emerge and disconnect into logical opposites is beautifully described in Buddhism by the term *vikalpa* which literally means "bifurcating conceptuality."

7. The distinction between "surface" and "deep" beliefs corresponds to the distinction between *parikalpita* and *sahaja* that is found in the Middle Path and other Buddhist philosophies.

8. Finally, the method of natural release is modelled on the Complete Fulfillment (rDzogs chen) concept of *rang grol. Rang grol* literally means "intrinsic freedom" or "self-liberated." Intrinsic freedom refers to the fact that the nature of mind *(sems nyid)*, or what is our real being *(chos nyid)*, is innately free, in the sense that it is unconstrained and uncontaminated by our circumstances and conditions. When we connect with the source of our being, we are intrinsically free because we feel spacious and liberated no matter what our external circumstances or internal condition may be. The term *rang grol* also refers to the capacity for constricting emotions and limiting beliefs to be liberated or freed from within themselves once they are experienced just as they are, without resistance. In other words, the real nature of our emotions and thoughts is to be free, spacious and unconstrained. We use the term natural release to refer to the self-liberating capacity of

thoughts and emotions and also to a gently effective method, used in the practical program, for harmonizing and thereby liberating conflicting beliefs and emotions.

APPENDIX TWO

The course

The authors have developed a practical, experiential course based on the principles and ideas outlined in this book. The course is offered residentially and non-residentially, and is usually conducted over seven consecutive days. Prior to commencing the course you engage in an informal group or individual session with a facilitator. This session gives you an opportunity to more deeply explore the principles outlined in this book, to ask questions and to discuss the value of this approach in your life.

The course cultivates an experience of authentic presence and intrinsic freedom by experientially deconstructing the primitive and pervasive belief that "something is wrong or missing" in our lives. This belief is recognized and dealt with in different frames of reference. For some people this belief is embedded within a material frame of reference which sees the cause of our suffering in terms of an absence of certain physical resources. For many people the belief that "something is missing" occurs within a psychological interpretation of the human condition which suggests that we are unhealthy or disturbed. The belief that "something is missing" can also be conditioned and supported by a spiritual world-view which sees us as impure or fallen. The belief also occurs within a philosophical frame of reference which views our problem as primarily one of ignorance.

As the belief that "something is missing" is gently and skillfully deconstructed, in whatever framework it appears, you are left with a simple and totally fresh experience of "what is." Within this experience the idea that anything could or should be different from how it is becomes quite absurd and meaningless. The mere attempt to construct the thought that things could be better becomes ludicrous. The result is a tremendous sense of freedom and spaciousness.

Course format

The format for the course is very flexible. You work in your own space and time, sharing an environment with other course members. The course is conducted in an honest and respectful atmosphere where the values of sharing and privacy are skillfully balanced. The group meets together once or twice a day for informal discussion.

The course is based on uncomplicated exercises which have been designed to enable you to connect with the source of your experience in a free and spacious way. These exercises follow a natural progression as they mirror the inner pathways leading to a state of real freedom and heightened presence.

The exercises are simple and easy to follow and the results are profound because they lead you to, and work at, the level of awareness where beliefs come into and go out of existence. The course thus gives ready access to a state of mind where conflicting thoughts, beliefs and emotions are automatically harmonized and naturally released.

Movement through the exercises is determined through discussion between you and a facilitator and is always individually tailored to your needs and experiences.

There are three main themes around which the exercises have been constructed. These are called the Practicals, Boundaries and Releases.

Practicals

In the Practicals you engage in a graduated set of simple yet powerful exercises that expand your awareness of your thoughts, feelings and environment. This leads to an experience of heightened presence and ease. During these exercises you get beneath your automatic, intellectual judgments about your thoughts and feelings and learn to appreciate a new smooth texture that connects, heightens and balances everything you experience.

Boundaries

Most conflict that we experience occurs in the form of interpersonal problems, as breakdowns between what we do (action) and who we are (being), and discontinuities between our beliefs and our experience. During this phase you work with the boundaries between these distinctions. You see how the distinctions are constructed between self and other, being and action, belief and experience, and how the boundaries which divide and separate them can be removed. This gives you much greater freedom and confidence in accepting a wider range of experiences.

Releases

In this phase of the course you learn a method called "natural release." This technique brings conflicting beliefs together and allows them to effortlessly dissolve away. You learn how to do this for beliefs which have limited you historically or which you anticipate will limit you in the future. You also learn how to apply this method in the here-and-now to dissolve thoughts and feelings that you believe shouldn't be happening to you. This produces an experience of intrinsic freedom which allows you to be authentically present and appreciative of whatever is being experienced.

The structure of the course ensures that you gain the ability and confidence to gracefully release restricting thoughts, emotions, fears and hopes across all of the important areas of your life, such as relationships, career, health and spirituality.

Integrating the course

All of the exercises in the course have been designed to "lubricate" your experiences, enabling you to readily appreciate how they are constructed. The exercises are viewed as powerful tools by course participants. However, if they are considered necessary and indispensable, there is the potential for conflict to occur.

Thus, during the course, the facilitators work with you to deconstruct any beliefs about needing to be doing specific exercises, to be in the environment of the course, or to be working with the facilitators themselves. This enables you to fully integrate the course experience in your work, family and leisure environments by seeing that there need be no division between the course and what comes after it. In so doing all concerns about losing the benefits of the course or needing to maintain one's sense of freedom and presence are deconstructed. In this way you go beyond the limitations of "doing a course." The result is even greater freedom and spaciousness. You can then simply be where you are—present to "what is" and intrinsically free.

INDEX

Index

FURTHER INFORMATION

For further information about Peter and Penny's practical work please contact:

Australasia

Intrinsic Freedom
23a Britten Street
Glen Iris
Victoria 3146
Australia
Phone + 61 3 885 0119
Facsimile + 61 3 885 3939

North America

Intrinsic Freedom
555 Bryant Street, # 302
Palo Alto
California 94301
USA
Phone + 1 408 973 9087
Facsimile + 1 408 973 9874